Come, Let Us Reason TOGETHER

Connecting with God through the Word

Mary Baird

5 Fold Media
Visit us at www.5foldmedia.com

Come, Let Us Reason Together
Copyright © 2013 by Mary Baird
Published by 5 Fold Media, LLC
www.5foldmedia.com

All rights reserved. No part of this book may be reproduced, stored in a retrieval system, or transmitted in any form or by any means-electronic, mechanical, photocopy, recording, or otherwise-without prior written permission of the copyright owner, except by a reviewer who wishes to quote brief passages in connection with a review for inclusion in a magazine, website, newspaper, podcast, or broadcast. Cover photography © Vibe Images-Fotolia.com The views and opinions expressed from the writer are not necessarily those of 5 Fold Media, LLC.

Scripture quotations taken from the New American Standard Bible®, Copyright © 1960, 1962, 1963, 1968, 1971, 1972, 1973, 1975, 1977, 1995 by The Lockman Foundation. Used by permission.

ISBN: 978-1-936578-53-5
Library of Congress Control Number: 2012956208

Dedication

This collection of writings was written to honor my Creator God. It is He who has given me whatever ability to write and to place upon paper the things He has so gracefully shown me from His Word. My prayer is that He will be honored in whatever way He wishes.

I also thank my husband and best friend, Jimmy, who encouraged me to pursue the publishing of my thoughts. In the many hours spent formulating all that is written on the following pages, he never once complained about my time sitting behind the computer. He read every page, gave me good observations, and desires the glory of God to be shown.

"Not to us, O Lord, not to us, but to Your name give glory because of Your lovingkindness, because of Your truth" (Psalms 115:1).

The Word of God

"For the word of God is living and active and sharper than any two-edged sword, and piercing as far as the division of soul and spirit, of both joints and marrow, and able to judge the thoughts and intentions of the heart" (Hebrews 4:12).

Are you a born-again Christian? If you answered yes, then I'll assume you believe this statement from the book of Hebrews. We don't fully understand the force of that verse; if we did, we'd spend daily time in the Word. But in point of fact, if you visit most churches on Sunday mornings, you'll find very few people who even carry a Bible. Worse still, you'll find many professing believers who know very little about that living and active document.

No other book has the power of the Bible. The Bible is the only book that claims the ability to see into the very heart and soul of a man and know everything about him. That one ability assures us that God knows our deepest needs and the exact actions required to accomplish our greatest good. The Bible is the supernatural work of the holy, sovereign Creator God. In the entire universe, of all the planets, God chose to put man on Earth and communicate with him.

If you're a Christian, my book is designed to encourage you to read and study Scripture. If you're not a Christian, then my challenge is for you to test this stunning letter from God and watch what happens in your life. May God's grace reveal His majesty and splendor, and may His heart of compassion flow into your life as you study and believe His words of love to us—the Bible.

Contents

Living a Square Life in a Round World	7
How Does Your Garden Grow?	15
Bewitched, Bothered, and Bewildered	17
Bathsheba, Wife of Uriah	19
The Bold and the Beautiful	22
El Roi	26
Debilitating Fear	29
Broken Bread	33
Was Jesus Politically Correct?	35
Sad Ending for a Rich King	37
So What's New?	41
A Harlot Meets Jehovah God	44
Will the Real Mother Please Stand Up?	49
Hang On, Saints	52
A Dirty Word	54
Muddy River	58
A Supercilious Woman	62
A Profitable Death	65
Disqualified	67
Bloodline	69
Do You Have Humility?	72
Our Honored Guest	74
Torn Curtain	76
Intelligent Love	78
When the Saints Go Marching In	81
Do You Have A Dagon?	84

Where Were You?	88
Faith Whiteout	91
The Portico of Solomon	94
Our Three Inch Rudder	96
By the Hair of Your Chinny Chin Chin	99
Divine Humor	102
Do You Know I AM?	105
Easter's Guarantee	107
Is Prosperity a Handicap?	109
Of Cattle and Kings	113
Lie from Hell	115
Proof Beyond Belief	119
Spiritual Babies	121
The Reluctant Saint	124
Love's Anguish	128
Which Way?	130
Pomp and Circumstance	132
More than Esther's Story	135
Pleasing Prayer	139
Foolish Things	143
Under His Wings	145
Burning Hearts	148
Oh, Be Quiet!	152
Our True Debt	154

Living a Square Life in a Round World

"And do not be conformed to this world, but be transformed by the renewing of your mind, so that you may prove what the will of God is, that which is good and acceptable and perfect" (Romans 12:2).

One of the first educational toys we gave our son was a square wooden puzzle with various shapes carved into the top. You had to fit wooden pieces into the correct shape on the board. I watched as my son tried to determine how the puzzle worked. He would take a square piece and try to place it into the round hole on the board. I would patiently take his hand and direct it to the space designed for the piece he held in his hand. A confident smile would cross his face when it perfectly fit into the spot. In no time, he had it down and could work the puzzle in seconds. In order to add some excitement, he delighted in purposefully trying to fit a piece into the wrong slot to see my reaction. When I caught on to what he was doing, it became a game for us. I'd pretend exasperation when he'd deliberately misdirect the pieces, and then he'd give me a mischievous grin and place it where it belonged.

Much as the pieces of that puzzle would not fit into the inappropriate slots, Christians cannot fit into the world system; in fact, we should not. And yet, we are seemingly asked to do just that.

Come, Let Us Reason Together

In our Lord's high priestly prayer, He makes an interesting statement. John 17:15-16 says, "I do not ask You [God] to take them [my disciples] out of the world, but to keep them from the evil one. They are not of the world, even as I am not of the world."

God had an assignment for His disciples, and He has an assignment for every believer. Otherwise the moment we were saved, He'd take us home. The trick is to be in the world but not of the world.

When I was a teenager, if a peer behaved in a manner not conforming to a particular mold, they were called a "square." It meant that the teen didn't choose to participate in certain "cool" activities and remained aloof. These squares were usually lonely, and I often felt sorry for them, but to reach out would have meant being labeled in the same manner. When I became a believer, God gave me the opportunity to find out what it means to be ostracized and misunderstood. I am now the square.

Getting Started

In order to live our lives as Christians in a world that considers us misguided at best and crazy at worst, we must understand some guidelines if we are to survive and carry out the work Jesus left us to do.

It is essential that we realize the magnanimous gift God has given us in Christ. We were a motley group of sinful people and we were certainly not seeking God. Our representative, Adam, had plunged man into a downward spiral of separation from their Creator. Man's future looked bleak indeed. How could a holy God ever reconcile with sinful men and remain holy? The entire Old Testament is a history of how God develops a bloodline leading to the Messiah. Living on this side of the cross, we can see clearly how Christ was the fulfillment of that bloodline, and how He answered all the needed criteria to die as our substitute and pay the price we owed to God. As Christ hung on the cross at Golgotha, sin was placed directly upon Him, and if we accept that payment, we are no longer under the penalty of eternal separation from God (Romans 8:1-2). As we come to fully appreciate who we are in Christ, living in a hostile world becomes easier.

Conformed or Transformed?

The writer to the Roman church gives believers the proper view, both negatively and positively, of how we are to conduct our lives in an unfriendly world, and yet remain separated. Read Romans 12:2 again. We are not to allow the world to pull us, push us, cram us, or lure us into its mold. That's not always easy; the world has some very enticing tools it uses, and not all the world offers is bad. Some of it is rather pleasant and satisfying.

Our major defense is in the mind. And in order to prove what the will of God is, we must study Scripture. God speaks to us today through His Word, and the more we know what it says, the better able we are to filter out truth from lies. If the world says one thing, but the Scriptures say another, which one are we to believe?

The mind of man is a fascinating organ, even in our fallen state. But our minds are also easily deceived and manipulated. Before the fall of man, as recorded in Genesis, Adam and Eve had perfect minds because sin had not entered their souls. The devil knew exactly how to approach Eve and twist her thinking until she made the fatal mistake of listening to lies. All Satan had to do was justify a reason for disobeying the command of God.

Come, Let Us Reason Together

There is no doubt that Satan has control of the world system. We realize that God permits such control, but the control is real. When Jesus was sent into the wilderness to be tempted after His baptism (Luke 4:1-2), Satan tried to goad Jesus into sin. After going without food for forty days, our Lord was tired, hungry, and thirsty. It was a perfect time for Satan to unleash his evil plan to throw Jesus off track. No one knew better than Satan who Jesus was and why He had come to earth. This would not be the last time Satan tried to interfere with the eternal plan of God.

One of the temptations was to offer Jesus all the kingdoms of the world if He would only worship Satan. It's interesting that Jesus didn't engage in an argument with him in regard to his offer being illegitimate; Jesus simply quoted Deuteronomy 6:13. I have always felt that we can never fully understand what was taking place between Jesus and Satan. We must remember that we are finite in nature and a conversation between the God of the universe and the most powerful fallen angel ever to exist cannot be comprehended completely. But we can appreciate that this was a legitimate offer and that our Lord persevered.

Since Satan has such power in the world, he can entice us with many offers that are pleasing to our senses and our desires. Some of those are pride, success, wealth, recognition, material possessions, sensuality, and worldly knowledge. All these things, when used for our selfish benefit, are designed to shape us so that we begin to fit perfectly into a mold not intended for believers.

There is a protection against conformity to the world. God has designed Satan's world system that even when believers try to look and act in a worldly behavior, the world still does not accept them. The Apostle John tells us in his first epistle, "Do not be surprised, brethren, if the world hates you" (1 John 3:13). If we can live a worldly life and not feel the pangs of uneasiness, we'd better take stock of our salvation.

Where Is Your Treasure?

You can tell a lot about a person by what he treasures, and you can tell what he treasures by listening to what he spends his time talking about. We all love our families, but when they become the center of our existence, we have moved beyond what God intended. We all love security, but when that becomes our all important goal, we have ceased to trust in the One who gives us all things to enjoy.

Jesus teaches an interesting concept in Matthew 6:19-21. He ends the instruction by saying, "for where your treasure is, there your heart will be also."

In the Apostle Paul's last known letter to his young convert, Timothy, Paul pours out his heart and soul. He knows his death is imminent and he wants to leave some last minute instructions to this young man who will carry on the battle of Christ. In a way, it's sad to see the apostle ending his life in a dark, dreary, cold dungeon after taking the salvation message to so many people.

At one time, Paul had many friends who stood behind him in the ministry, but at this point of his life, many had deserted him in his hour of need. Don't misunderstand. Paul would not have changed places with anyone, and he was looking forward to seeing his Lord, but there is something heartbreaking when you hear his words. At one time a man named Demas had been a source of comfort to Paul. No doubt, this man had supported Paul and stood beside him as a fellow believer and lover of the good news. Perhaps he had even supported Paul financially. The tough work of evangelism requires having friends around to encourage and strengthen us. But something happened to Demas. We don't know exactly what caused him to abandon Paul, but we are told in 2 Timothy 4:10 that Demas "having loved this present world" deserted Paul.

I'm not sure if Demas was a true believer, but when I get to heaven I would like to ask him if his abandonment of truth for the world was worth it. I think I know what he'd say, don't you?

One man who did leave an enormous life of riches and honor was Moses. It's recorded in the book of Hebrews 11:23-26 that Moses was willing to endure ill treatment at the hands of the Egyptians rather than to enjoy the passing pleasures of sin. Further, it says Moses considered the reproach of Christ greater riches than the treasures of Egypt. Now that's what I call putting your life where your treasure is.

Help for the Weary

I think we can all agree that walking the Christian life is not a solitary profession. There are times when the issues of life come crashing down around our heads and leave us reeling with worry, frustration, and a feeling of helplessness. Our Lord designed the church as a place of refreshment and renewing of our spirits. As we meet together to obey the commands of Christ in the taking of the Lord's Supper, baptism of new believers, and the study of God's Word, we realize we are not alone. We know Christ is always with us, but sometimes we need warm bodies that laugh with us, cry with us, pray out loud for us, encourage us, come to our aid in times of trouble, and a myriad of other supports.

Mary Baird

In the book of Hebrews, the writer says, "Not forsaking our own assembling together, as is the habit of some, but encouraging one another; and all the more, as you see the day drawing near" (Hebrews 10:25). Bible teachers have debated exactly what day the writer means, but one thing we can know, if the day was close some 2,000 years ago, what about now?

The local church is to be a light in a dark world. We've been given various gifts by the Holy Spirit in order to carry out the work God leaves us here to do. It's in the church that we perfect our gifts so that we can go forward and use them in our neighborhoods, our schools, and the workplace.

Everyone loves to be a winner. I know I do, but I can count the times I've actually won anything on one hand. For the times I've lost, I need more than my ten fingers. If you want to be on a winning side that you can be sure will triumph, then the universal church is the place for you. Our Lord gave us the assurance, "I will build My church; and the gates of Hades will not overpower it" (Matthew 16:18b). The reason the church will win is because Christ Himself is building it. How sure is that?

Where Are You Going?

My husband and I have been a little slow in entering into all the technology of the last decade, so we have only recently started using a GPS system for traveling. In fact, our children gave it to us as a gift. I guess they figured it would be another decade before we decided to purchase one of our own. We used it on a recent trip, and have continued to sing the praises of a system that can guide you anywhere you wish to go, and even correct your mistake if you should take a wrong turn.

As a believer, we never need to wonder where we're going since Jesus Christ is our GPS tracking system. In Philippians

3:20, Paul tells us that, "For our citizenship is in heaven, from which also we eagerly wait for a Savior, the Lord Jesus Christ."

If we understand this reality, we would understand that in truth, we are not citizens of the nation in which we live. We are not citizens of the world or citizens of the universe. Our citizenship is in heaven with our Lord, and we are to eagerly wait for our appointed hour to be transported there. Paul also tells us in his letter to the Ephesian church, "So then you [believers] are no longer strangers and aliens, but you are fellow citizens with the saints, and are of God's household" (Ephesians 2:19).

At one time, we were citizens of Satan's empire and destined to spend eternity with him, but now we've been declared citizens of Christ's empire. What a marvelous truth and one that should cause great encouragement and determination for us to stay focused on our spiritual walk.

Conclusion

No one said that living a square life in a round world would be easy. The Lord made it clear what a commitment to Him entailed. If we go back to a letter written to Timothy, Paul says, "Indeed, all who desire to live godly in Christ Jesus will be persecuted" (2 Timothy 3:12). I don't think you can be any clearer than that. Is it worth it? You'll have to make that decision. All I can say is that in my many years on this earth, the world has seldom lived up to its promises or expectations. For me, I'll take my chances with the sovereign God of the universe.

How Does Your Garden Grow?

"But grow in the grace and knowledge of our Lord and Savior Jesus Christ. To Him be the glory, both now and to the day of eternity. Amen" (2 Peter 3:18).

There's an old English jingle that asks Mary how her garden grows. The reply is with silver bells, cockle shells, and little maids in a row.[1] I've often wished I had a dollar for every time someone quoted me that little jingle. I suppose when your name is Mary, you should expect that.

Everyone knows that a garden could not possibly grow with those items. They would make great garden decorations, but that's about it. What you need is water, sunshine, fertilizer, and "TLC"—tender loving care. Not that I'm an expert on gardens, but even a novice knows that.

Our spiritual life also needs certain things to grow. It takes more than silver bells, cockle shells, and little maids all in a row. Or to say it another way, it takes more than merely going to Church, singing hymns, and carrying a Bible.

Water in Scripture refers to both the Holy Spirit (John 7:37-39), and the Word of God (Ephesians 5:25-26). In order to plant the garden of our spiritual life, we must first be reborn

---
1. Original author unknown.

by the Holy Spirit through Christ, then we begin to grow by a continuous and generous watering of the Word of God. Next, we need the Son-shine—Christ (John 1:4). Without daily fellowship with Him, we live in darkness, cannot grow, and die. The fertilizer is a bit more troublesome. Fertilizer is not pleasant or pretty; it stinks, but it is absolutely necessary for growth. Our spiritual life must have periods of trials and problems to give us maximum results (James 1:12). Even Jesus learned obedience through the things which he suffered (Hebrews 5:8). Here is the best part—God gives us the TLC we need all the days of our lives (2 Corinthians 1:3-4). He comforts us when we are worn out from a world that is hostile toward us, and He holds us when we are too tired to press on (Psalms 63:6-8).

Paul contrasts those who distort the Scriptures and cause others to stumble, with those who are aware and on guard for false teachers. Paul goes on to admonish believers by saying, "But grow in the grace and knowledge of our Lord and Savior Jesus Christ" (2 Peter 3:18a). May our spiritual garden become a fragrant aroma to our Savior.

Bewitched, Bothered, and Bewildered

> "You foolish Galatians, who has bewitched you, before whose eyes Jesus Christ was publicly portrayed as crucified? This is the only thing I want to find out from you: did you receive the Spirit by the works of the Law, or by hearing with faith? Are you so foolish? Having begun by the Spirit, are you now being perfected by the flesh?" (Galatians 3:1-3).

Have you ever known anyone who could never be pleased? It may have been a boss or a family member. No matter what you did, it was never good enough to win their approval. I fear many children have grown up with parents who could not bring themselves to acknowledge total acceptance of their child. How sad it is that those children go through life trying to please everyone, never feeling they succeed.

Even sadder is the fact that many believers live their Christian lives trying to please a god who can never be satisfied. The Apostle Paul ran into that with the church in Galatia. Some false teachers had bothered the Galatian believers saying they had to obey the law in order to be right with Jehovah God. They were called "Judaizers" and believed that the Old Testament law still needed to be followed in order to secure their salvation. Paul was furious when he wrote his letter reminding them that this was not his teaching. Paul had taught them that their salvation was by grace through the work of

Come, Let Us Reason Together

Jesus Christ on the cross. Man's works added nothing. If I may ask a question: If Paul, who once followed the law of Moses, came to understand that now man comes to God through grace and not works, do you think any man-made requirements today hold any weight with God?

There is nothing more bewildering than trying to follow a harsh taskmaster god. You never know where you stand with a god like that. One day you may feel you do well; the next day you mess up and have that gnawing feeling of disapproval. The distinguishing beauty of Christianity that separates it from all other religious systems is our security in Christ. Because He paid all the dues owed by us, we are free to follow our God in complete assurance of His acceptance.

So the next time someone tries to convince you that you must follow certain rules in order to maintain and keep your salvation, tell them that since you had nothing to do with your deliverance, then you have nothing to do with keeping it. Tell them when Christ said, "It is finished" as he hung on the cross, that's exactly what He meant. Tell them that the penalty for sin has been paid in full and all anyone can do is accept that provision. Tell them that if they want to live in bondage to insecurity, bewilderment, and doubt, rather than enjoy freedom in Christ, they can go right ahead.

Bathsheba, Wife of Uriah

> "Then it happened in the spring, at the time when kings go out to battle, that David sent Joab and his servants with him and all Israel, and they destroyed the sons of Ammon and besieged Rabbah. But David stayed at Jerusalem" (2 Samuel 11:1).

The messenger stood before David in the royal palace. His breathing was labored because of the hasty run from the siege against Rabbah in Ammon. "My master, the battle against Rabbah was fierce, but your captain, Joab, pressed the enemy into the city. Joab instructed me to tell you that in ordering our men to venture so close to the wall, many were killed by the arrows being hurled at us from above. He also instructed me to tell you that Uriah is dead."

David stood silent for a moment and then said softly. "Tell Joab to press the city further and do not concern himself with the losses. Battle takes one as well as another. Tell him that I'm confident he can take Rabbah and win the victory."

The messenger obediently nodded and hurried out. David called for his servant and commanded him to go to the home of Uriah and tell Bathsheba that her husband was dead. "Tell her that when her days of mourning are completed, she will become my wife." David dismissed his servant as the weight of what he had done began to penetrate his soul.

***

Come, Let Us Reason Together

Have you ever sinned during a moment of passion only to regret your actions when the consequences of those actions became apparent? You may also have tried to remedy the first action by plotting another equally bad solution. David had lusted after another man's wife, Bathsheba. She was pregnant by David, and as an adulteress, the Jewish law called for her death. David knew that to save her life and reputation, he needed to make it look as if the baby belonged to her husband, Uriah. He was one of David's brave soldiers who was completely loyal to his king and had been on the battle field for weeks. No matter how hard David tried to get him to abandon his post and go to his wife, Uriah stubbornly refused. He did not want to leave his men for the gratification of home.

The plot began to thicken and now David was desperate. He instructed his commander, Joab, to place Uriah in front of the fiercest battle so that he would be killed; then Bathsheba would be free to marry him. It worked exactly as David had planned and he did marry Bathsheba. However, the cost of this abomination would be heavy.

One other interesting note about this incident is that from the time David married Bathsheba, whenever she is mentioned in Scripture, God reminds us that she was the wife of Uriah. In Matthew 1:6 in the genealogy of Christ it says, "Jesse was the father of David the king. David was the father of Solomon by Bathsheba who had been the wife of Uriah."

In Psalms 51, David cries out to God for forgiveness of this sin, and God does forgive him, but it costs David his child and nearly his kingdom. It should remind us that we can never hide our sins from God, and there is often a price to pay even after we confess and are forgiven. There are consequences for what we do, and most often, the sin which we commit hastily for a short time leaves us with years of regret.

David is able to write in Psalms 103:10-12, "He (God) has not dealt with us according to our sins, nor rewarded us according to our iniquities. For as high as the heavens are above the earth, so great is His lovingkindness toward those who fear Him. As far as the east is from the west, so far has He removed our transgressions from us."

David knew that nothing could separate him from the love of God, and today believers have even more reason to feel secure. The Apostle Paul reminds us in his letter to the Romans (Romans 8:35-39) that nothing can separate us from the love of Christ.

The Bold and the Beautiful

"Then David said to Abigail, 'Blessed be the Lord God of Israel, who sent you this day to meet me, and blessed be your discernment, and blessed be you, who have kept me this day from bloodshed and from avenging myself by my own hand'" (1 Samuel 25:32-33).

Abigail was as strikingly beautiful as she was wise—this wife and mistress of Nabal's household. Her raven hair flowed around her shoulders and down her back in graceful cascades, and her ivory skin was flawless. From her emerald green eyes came a look of gentleness, and her winsome smile charmed anyone in her company.

Her one misfortune was the arranged marriage to her husband, Nabal. Since Nabal was an extremely prosperous man, Abigail's family felt pleased with the union. But Nabal was a contemptible, selfish, and brutish man who treated everyone with disdain—including his wife. He was known as the Maon—fool.

Knowing his habit of placing the family in precarious situations from his ugly dealings with others, Abigail was not surprised when her trusted servant, Silas, came running to the barn and told her about a perilous situation. Abigail was nursing a sick lamb in the barn when Silas brought her the news.

"My mistress," Silas took a heavy breath and continued. "May I speak frankly?"

Abigail glanced up at the servant. "Of course, Silas, what's wrong?"

"Mistress, some men came to our master, Nabal, to tell him that while we were grazing the sheep in Carmel they protected the shepherds from robbers as we were shearing the sheep. They acted as a wall around us the whole time we were there—we had no fear from anyone. The men asked for nothing in return for this protection but did this duty in response to their leader's instructions. Now they have come to our master's house at the request of their leader with an appeal. The men demanded nothing but only such as our master could spare." Silas fell silent.

"Yes, go on." Abigail prodded.

"Mistress, our master turned them away in disgrace and impugned the name of their leader. He sent them away empty handed. Adad and I tried to talk to our master and warn him of what would happen because of his actions, but he won't listen. These men and their leader will return, and I fear none of us will be safe."

"What is the leader's name?" Abigail asked hesitantly.

"His name is David." The look on the face of Silas told Abigail all she needed to know.

"May Yahweh give me strength to save us!" Abigail grabbed the arm of Silas. "Hurry! Tell Adina and Claudia to prepare bread, wine, dressed sheep, raisins, cakes of figs and roasted grain. Load them on donkeys and meet me back at the barn. Tell no one else of our mission. Run, run!"

Within an hour, the donkeys were loaded and ready to deliver the food to David and his men. Abigail had heard about David.

Come, Let Us Reason Together

By some he was considered a fugitive, but to most he was a hero that would someday be king of Israel. King Saul knew David was favored by God and that David would replace him on the throne. Saul had been chasing David throughout Israel but could never catch him. David and his men were elusive and formidable warriors, but David would not face Saul in battle because he respected the king's office. Abigail had heard how David and his men were champions for the Jewish people and protected them from outside enemies when they could. She also knew that to spurn his request for needed food for his men would be met with swift action.

Abigail mounted a donkey and instructed Silas to lead the way and that she would follow. They traveled a road toward an area where David might be lodging and hoped to find him in time to avoid tragedy. As she descended down the hidden part of the mountain, the sound of running horses coming in the opposite direction made her stop abruptly. The sound grew closer and Abigail saw several hundred men coming toward her at great speed. David raised his hand when he saw Abigail and the riders reined to a stop. She knew this was David and his men, swords strapped to their sides, and ready for battle with her husband Nabal.

Abigail dismounted, ran to David and bowed low before him. "On me alone, my lord, be the blame. And please let your maidservant speak to you, and listen to the words of your maidservant" (1 Samuel 25:24).

***

If you've read the story of David and Abigail, you know what happens, if you've not read the story, you'll enjoy it. Everything that makes for a good read is in this story—a beautiful woman, a handsome warrior, intrigue, bravery, romance—it's an exciting narrative. But it's more than just a good story. What can we learn from Abigail and David? I think the answer may be found in what David says to Abigail after she confronts him. Abigail took her life in her hands to stop a slaughter that might have had repercussions not only to herself, but also to David—the future king of Israel. Read the entire story and see what you come away with.

El Roi

"Now it came about, as she continued praying before the Lord, that Eli was watching her mouth. As for Hannah, she was speaking in her heart, only her lips were moving, but her voice was not heard. So Eli thought she was drunk" (1 Samuel 1:12-13).

Eli the priest became more irritated by the minute. The woman was obviously drunk and embarrassing herself before the God of Israel. *Imagine falling down drunk at the doorway of the temple,* Eli mused. In total disgust, Eli at last made the decision to remove her from his sight. "How long will you make yourself drunk?" he said with a loud voice. "Put away your wine from you." He motioned with his hands for her to leave.

The woman looked up in dismay. Tears were streaming down her face. She struggled to her feet and turned to face the old priest. Her voice trembled as she tried to form the words. "No, my lord, I am a woman oppressed in spirit; I have drunk neither wine nor strong drink, but I have poured out my soul before the Lord."

The woman was Hannah and her husband was Elkanah. Her nemesis, Peninnah, had many children, but Hannah was childless. Elkanah had assured Hannah that of his two wives she was his favorite, but that brought little comfort to Hannah. Peninnah continually provoked Hannah by reminding her that she could have no children. This fact would send her into hiding so that no one could see her tears. On each trip the family made to Shiloh to worship Yahweh, Hannah would present her plea to God for a child.

"Do not consider your maidservant as a worthless woman," Hannah continued. "For I have spoken until now out of my great concern and provocation."

Eli came closer to Hannah and realized she was not drunk. She was a woman in great distress and earnestly praying for an answer from the Lord. Hannah stepped back and pulled her veil across her face. Her head lowered in humble respect for Eli.

"Go in peace," Eli said tenderly, "and may the God of Israel grant your petition that you have asked of Him."

***

I've been friends with three barren women. All three had one thing in common: They longed for a child in a way I could never understand because having children for me was easy.

I found a verse in Psalms 113:9 that says, "He makes the barren woman abide in the house as a joyful mother of children. Praise the Lord!" I wrote the names of all three friends beside that verse to pray for them. Year after year each continued to see doctors, receive treatment, and lose babies. I've been able to check off two of those names and hold their babies in my arms. I continue to pray for the third and I know God will answer that prayer in His timing and in His way.

Our story of Hannah is interesting because we are told in 1 Samuel 1:5 that the Lord had closed her womb. I wonder why He did that. We can have an opinion, but we won't know for sure until eternity. The beauty of the story is that Hannah never stopped praying and never gave up, and we are told in 1 Samuel 1:19 that the Lord remembered her and she bore a child.

We all have areas in our life that we've presented to the Lord over and over, but nothing seems to happen. El Roi is a name for God meaning "God sees me." You can find the concept of that name in a story found in Genesis 16:13. No matter what your situation or need might be, God sees you. He knows your deepest desires. Trust Him and He will answer you with the best possible solution at the best possible time.

Debilitating Fear

"For you have not received a spirit of slavery leading to fear again, but you have received a spirit of adoption as sons by which we cry out, 'Abba! Father!'" (Romans 8:15).

There's a story told in my family about an incident between my mother and her aunt when my mother was only nine years old. The story goes as follows:

It was a warm early summer day in 1914 in the small town where my mother, Jennie Mae, was raised. Her unmarried Aunt Grace had packed a lunch of fried chicken, buttered bread, and hard boiled eggs. The two were headed for a picnic in a wooded area located on the other side of the numerous rows of railroad tracks. As they walked to their destination, my mother was skipping up and down in front of Grace. Her long red curls danced behind her and her dress swung back and forth around her legs. There was no worry about traffic in this rustic community at midday, so Grace gave her niece as much freedom as possible.

As they approached the hub of the railroad tracks, Grace surveyed in each direction and saw no trains making their way toward the terminal, but she reminded Jennie Mae to slow down and make sure to watch before running across. With a mischievous grin and a quick glance back at Grace, Jennie

Come, Let Us Reason Together

Mae took off in a mad dash across the tracks. "That little scalawag," Grace muttered to herself, "she never minds me."

Grace's ears picked up a sound of which she was all too familiar having lived her life in this bustling railroad town. It was the sorrowful sounding whistle of a train announcing its arrival. Grace glanced down the tracks and saw a train making the bend leading to the round house. She then glanced at Jennie Mae and realized her niece was paying no attention to the sound or image of the train. Grace shouted with every ounce of breath she had, but became painfully aware that not only was Jennie Mae not listening to her, but the train and Jennie Mae were on a collision course.

The engineer saw the little girl and gave another long blow of his whistle. This time Jennie Mae looked up and saw the train. She was running too fast to stop so the only option was to jump the track ahead of the train. Grace stood frozen in time and later said it was as if everything moved in slow motion. Each stride that Jennie Mae took brought her closer to an impact with the train. Jennie Mae took a giant leap and disappeared behind the massive black train engine as it roared by. Grace fell to the ground in a fainted heap. When Grace revived, her niece was standing over her along with a crowd of railroad men who had witnessed the near catastrophe. The back hem of Jennie Mae's dress was smeared with black smut from the engine of the train; it had missed her by inches.

That story was told many times as our family gathered for a meal. Grace said she had never felt fear as she did in those few moments before Jennie Mae made her jump. She couldn't move or speak, and her heart was pounding so fast she thought it would jump out of her chest. It was the most debilitating fear she'd ever experienced.

Mary Baird

Fear is like that and all of us have faced fears of one kind or another. Fear is a hard taskmaster and demands all our energy. It robs us of the joy and peace God desires for us. And following behind fear is worry. Between fear and worry, we waste a lot of vitality that could be spent in a much more productive way.

On the last night our Lord spent with His disciples in the upper room, Jesus told them that He was giving them peace (John 14:27). His peace, He said, would not be like the world's peace—temporary and based on circumstances. Christ told his disciples, "Do not let your heart be troubled; believe in God, believe also in me" (John 14:1). The peace we have as believers is based on the object of our faith: Christ and His promises.

If we have received Christ as our Savior and have trusted Him with our future, there is no reason for fear. The Apostle John in 1 John 4:18 says, "There is no fear in love; but perfect love casts out fear, because fear involves punishment, and the one who fears is not perfected in love." In fact, one of the fruits of the Spirit, as given in the book of Galatians, is peace. If we are placing our eternal welfare in the hands of God, it should follow that anything here on earth is temporary and does not deserve our fear.

There is a godly fear that we should have. In Proverbs 1:7, we are told that true wisdom must begin with a healthy fear of God. Christ Himself told us not to fear those who can kill us physically, but cannot kill the soul, but to fear Him (God) who is able to destroy both soul and body in hell (Matthew 10:28). And Hebrews 10:31 tell us that it is a fearful thing to fall into the hands of the living God. But proper fear sets us free to live a life pleasing to our heavenly Father. In Romans 8:15 we are told not to retreat back to our lives of fear because we have received a spirit of adoption. We have been adopted by God and we belong to His family.

Does this mean that we will never know fear? Not at all, for we are but human and there is much in this world to cause us fear—earthquakes, floods, tornados, wars, and a worldwide financial collapse just to name a few. Even the Apostle Paul in his letter to the Corinthian church told them that he had come to them in much fear and trembling to preach the Word of God (1 Corinthians 2:3). But we should not allow such fear to dominate or stifle our work here on earth.

Perhaps the verses that have meant most to me throughout my walk with the Lord, and have brought me back many times from the deep pit of fear and worry are found in Philippians 4:6-7, "Be anxious for nothing, but in everything by prayer and supplication with thanksgiving let your requests be made known to God. And the peace of God, which surpasses all comprehension, will guard your hearts and your minds in Christ Jesus." These are powerful words that can penetrate our hearts and cause us to rejoice. They contrast a life lived in anxiety and cause a life lived in peace. They tell us that we are to bring all those fears and worries to the throne room of grace, and that Christ will calm our hearts and guard us from stressful thoughts. How blessed we are to have a Savior who is able to sympathize with our weaknesses and to keep us secure in His love (Hebrews 4:15-16).

Broken Bread

> "They began to relate their experiences on the road and how He [Jesus] was recognized by them in the breaking of the bread" (Luke 24:35).

Have you ever walked into a bakery when they were taking hot bread from the oven? It's one of the sweetest aromas I know. Bread, they say, is the staff of life, and no matter where you go in the world, some kind of bread will be served.

While Jesus walked this earth, there were many times that He gave an analogy between literal bread, which is necessary to life, and Himself. In John 6:35, Jesus tells those listening that He is the bread of life and that anyone who partakes of Him will never hunger. Jesus compares Himself to the manna that God provided to the Israelites in the desert. The primary difference was that manna offered only temporary life, but when we partake of Him, we have eternal life.

What we understand today is that when He broke the bread the night He was betrayed, it symbolized His sacrificial giving of Himself. That night Jesus said, "This is my body which is given for you" (Luke 22:19). We symbolize that fact each time we break the bread as we observe the Lord's Supper.

Our story in Luke is about two men traveling to Emmaus, depressed because they had witnessed the crucifixion of the one they thought was the Messiah. They didn't recognize Jesus when He joined them on the road. When they approached the village where they were going, they insisted that Jesus join them for the night since it was getting dark, and traveling at night alone was dangerous. Jesus agreed and went into the house. As they reclined at the table to eat the evening meal, Jesus took bread and broke it.

As if blinders were removed from the two men's eyes, they now recognized their Master. Beyond the fact that it was God who opened their eyes, we are not told why the breaking of bread was the key. Perhaps they saw the nail pierced hands, or perhaps Jesus had a unique way of dividing and sharing bread. Jesus didn't spend the night. He disappeared before their eyes! Without delay, those two men returned to Jerusalem in victory to declare the resurrected Christ.

In the early church, the Lord's Supper was celebrated every week. I have heard people say that celebrating it so often causes it to become just another ritual and lose importance. To that I must disagree. If those who claim to be believers truly understand the significance and implications of that shared meal, it will never be reduced to mere formality. We should come away from the Lord's Table just as those two disciples did—in a hurry to tell others that Jesus is alive.

Was Jesus Politically Correct?

"Then the disciples came and said to Him [Jesus], 'Do You know that the Pharisees were offended when they heard this statement?'" (Matthew 15:12).

I'm the type of person who likes to feel accepted. Going against the flow has never been a desire of mine. Most people respond as I do—when in a crowd of people we tend to keep silent even when we disagree with the consensus of the majority. This shyness to express a controversial view now has a popular name. It's called political correctness. Sometimes this term has been a good thing, but more times than not, it's used as a tool to control speech and thought.

Jesus didn't worry about what was acceptable. In the days of Jesus, there was another word for political correctness. It was called tradition, and a Jew simply did not cross tradition even when it was evil. Jesus stayed in hot water most of the time because he broke with the traditions when they were wrong.

In Matthew 15:1-14, Jesus confronted the religious leaders in regard to their hypocritical observances of the Mosaic Law. They had twisted the commands to fit their own ungodly desires and then lashed out at Jesus for calling them out on it. What they were doing was shameful—a sin and a disgrace to the name of Jehovah God.

Even worse, because the religious leaders practiced such wickedness, it caused the Jewish people to adopt the same practices. Notice how even the disciples of Jesus reprimand Him for daring to speak the truth to these pompous leaders of the people.

Many of the sinful practices around us have become normalized by society because Christians have taken the easy road and kept silent. Deep down in our hearts, most of us realize that many of the things society has adopted as acceptable are seen in Scripture as reprehensible. An account of one man who spoke out in the Gospels is John the Baptist. He dared confront a half-Jewish Roman ruler regarding his sinful lifestyle. John was put to death for speaking out.

Christ has called us to be witnesses to the truth even when it means going against the crowd. God has not changed His mind regarding right and wrong. False deities may change their minds depending on their mood, but not so with our Sovereign. Man may try and twist what God has affirmed; they may say that we are in a new era and we should discard outdated rules. But God's Word regarding sin has never changed and neither should ours.

Sad Ending for a Rich King

"I have seen all the works which have been done under the sun, and behold, all is vanity and striving after wind" (Ecclesiastes 1:14).

If you're the kind of person who enjoys knowing the ending of a book before you read it, you'll absolutely love the book of Ecclesiastes in the Old Testament. Solomon, who wrote the book during his declining years, tells us right up front what the manuscript is all about. In the beginning verses, he says, "Vanity of vanities! All is vanity" (Ecclesiastes 1:2).

Solomon was the richest man who ever lived, or perhaps who will ever live. Just to get an idea of how wealthy this man was, read 1 Kings 10:14-29. If you think Bill Gates is rich, just check out King Solomon.

Solomon was the king of Israel during the nation's most glorious and prosperous days. He was the son of King David and Solomon took the throne when his father was dying. The first part of Solomon's reign was remarkable. God was pleased with his humility and his concern for the people, so God granted him wisdom beyond any man who had ever lived. He ruled with unparalleled intelligence. Dignitaries came from all over the world to hear Solomon's wisdom and to question him regarding significant issues.

But something happened to Solomon in his later years, and he became a bitter and disillusioned man. One thing he did give us though—he showed us that having money will not bring lasting pleasure or contentment if used wrongly. Those of us who don't have a great deal of money don't really believe that, but here was a man who had the means to experiment with every kind of imagined nirvana to find happiness. And what was his conclusion? All was vanity!

Let's look at some of the experiments Solomon tried. He started out using his God given wisdom to learn as much as he could. In other words, he obtained several PhDs. His conclusion is found in Ecclesiastes 1:18, "Because in much wisdom there is much grief, and increasing knowledge results in increasing pain." Have you ever seen an educated fool? They're people who have spent so much time in books that they have no common sense for living.

Solomon's next experiment is a common practice today. He tried a life devoted to pleasure. He said, why not drink until drunk and see how that will affect his mind; he says he took hold of folly. It doesn't say (and I'm happy it doesn't) what the folly was, but I think I can imagine. We're told in Ecclesiastes 2:8 that Solomon had many concubines.

When pleasure left him unfulfilled, he decided that being creative was the ticket. He built many lavish houses and planted vineyards and gardens. He made parks with all kinds of fruit trees. He made ponds to irrigate all his vegetation and planted forests. He acquired massive herds of sheep and cattle and had hundreds of servants to tend to all his possessions and to his own personal needs. On top of that, he amassed silver and gold by the tons. He had his own entertainment—professional singers and dancers just for his personal enjoyment. His conclusion for this effort was, "Thus I considered all my activities which my hands had done and the labor which I had exerted, and behold all was vanity and striving after wind and there was no profit under the sun" (Ecclesiastes 2:11). There is some humor here. Solomon looked around at all he had built and all his possessions and realized that he'd have to leave all his "stuff" behind for his children. He may have known what kind of children he'd raised and knew they'd probably be fools and squander everything he'd worked so hard to accumulate. Sound familiar? I've come in contact with some wealthy people who feared what their children would do once they were dead.

Next Solomon moves into that portion of his experiments evidenced by contemplating life around him. He realizes that where there should be justice and righteousness, there is wickedness. He wonders why anyone does anything because we all must die and return to the dust from which we came. He sees that most of the world resides under oppression from ruthless leaders and there is no one to help them. Men who at one time were rich and prosperous lost everything from a bad investment and they had no children to support them in their older years. Not only that, but when a man dies, even if he has riches, he can't take any of it with him and leaves this life exactly as he came into it—naked.

Are you depressed yet? Hang in there because this brilliant and wise man finally sees what's important in this life to bring us contentment. After more observances, Solomon boils life down to just a few words. Chapter 12 is the culmination to all his searching. In Ecclesiastes 12:1-6 he describes the aging process that every man will experience if he lives long enough. He urges us to remember our Creator when we're young because it gets harder to believe as we age. Solomon encourages us to listen to men of God (wise men) because they goad us into right living and their words are like well driven nails. These wise men and what they teach us are from one Shepherd who we know as Jesus Christ.

"The conclusion" says the "Preacher" (Solomon), "when all has been heard, is: fear God and keep His commandments, because this applies to every person" (Ecclesiastes 12:13). At least Solomon finally came back to the importance of a relationship with God—and that happiness will never be lasting apart from God. How sad that a man who began as God's man decided he knew better how to enjoy life and used the gifts given him for himself. We don't have to be rich to get off base, do we? Many times we too think we know better than God how to make the most of this life. How sad that we see so many Christians take all God has given them and use it for their own pleasure. Our Lord said it best as recorded in Mark 8:36, "For what does it profit a man to gain the whole world, and forfeit his soul?"

So What's New?

> "Remember my affliction and my wandering, the wormwood and bitterness. Surely my soul remembers and is bowed down within me. This I recall to my mind, therefore I have hope. The Lord's lovingkindnesses indeed never cease, for His compassions never fail. They are new every morning; great is Your faithfulness. 'The Lord is my portion,' says my soul, 'Therefore I have hope in Him'" (Lamentations 3:19-24).

The Preacher in the book of Ecclesiastes says, "there is nothing new under the sun" (Ecclesiastes 1:9b). He may be right about 99 percent of most things, but there is one particular Scripture that proves him incorrect.

I hate to admit this, but I'm a proficient worrier. I don't say that with pride since worry is a sin before God. Worry indicates that you don't trust in a sovereign God who is in control; nothing happens outside His plan and purpose. We may not always like His plan and purpose at the time, but Scripture tells us everything will work out for God's glory and our good (Romans 8:28). In Ephesians 5:20, we read, "Always giving thanks for all things in the name of our Lord Jesus Christ to God, even the Father." Do you think it really means "all things"? That verse gives many of us a hard time, doesn't it?

As I've grown older, my worry has taken on a new dimension. I imagine it's because I now have a better understanding of all the variables of life. It seems that at bedtime—when my attentions are not engaged—my worries strike. In the shadows of night when all is silent and my mind is free from the busyness of the day, I can begin to formulate all kinds of possibilities for the future. My sleep is interrupted; I have feelings of guilt; my mind gets no rest; and then anger sets in. Praise God that most of the time I'm able to commit the night to God, roll over, and go to sleep.

I can identify with the writer of the book of Lamentations. The name actually tells us the nature of the book—lamenting about everything. Whoever the writer was, he looked at life with eyes wide open and he saw trouble all around him. He was a man who didn't live in fantasy land. Or to put it another way—he lived in reality. He probably wasn't much fun to be around because we humans don't always want to look at things through the eyes of reality. I think that's why we love entertainment. It helps us escape from the uncomfortable facts of living in a sinful world.

But situated in the middle of Lamentations is a statement of impeccable truth. The statement has meant much to me because on those nights when my worry keeps me from the sleep I need, I have experienced these verses to be provably true. Reread Lamentations 3:19-24.

I would tell Solomon, who wrote Ecclesiastes, that he needed to make one exception to his statement of nothing new. God's lovingkindness, His compassions, and His faithfulness are *new* every morning. Isn't that beautiful? Every morning we start fresh and new. We can confess our sin of worry and head off for the day knowing our God will give us renewal in our inner mind and spirit. I've experienced it many times in my own life.

Mary Baird

The next time you've had a particularly bad day and gone to bed feeling exhausted, frustrated, defeated, and fearful, just remember that when you open your eyes the next morning, God is there with a fresh new ocean full of hope. It's free for the taking.

A Harlot Meets Jehovah God

"Then Joshua the son of Nun sent two men as spies secretly from Shittim, saying, 'Go, view the land, especially Jericho.' So they went and came into the house of a harlot whose name was Rahab, and lodged there" (Joshua 2:1).

Akim and Zollie stood motionless and pulled their tunics lower over their faces. They had sought safety in a lonely passageway trying to shake the shadowy figure following them, but to no avail. Now cornered, the two men turned to face their supposed adversary. Both reached for the daggers they carried in their belts. "What do you want?" Akim asked harshly. "Why are you following us?"

The mysterious figure pulled the veil from her head. "I'm here to help you." She said in a frantic whisper. "You are in dire danger. The king knows you've come to Jericho to spy out the city for defeat and he has men looking for you." Even in the dimly lit passage, the men could make out a woman standing before them. She moved closer. "You're Hebrews, aren't you?" Her tone of voice was almost reverent. "Come and follow me, and I'll put you someplace safe for now." The woman returned her veil and headed for the opening in the passage. She turned to see if the men were following her. "Why are you standing there? Please—you must trust me. We don't have much time." The woman raised her hand and motioned for the men to come. "I'll explain everything when you're safe."

Akim and Zollie looked at each other then back at the woman standing in the opening. Akim tilted his head toward his companion and softly asked, "What do you think, Zollie?"

Akim continued watching the woman cautiously. "I'm not sure, Akim. Why would this woman want to help us? She may lead us into a trap."

"Could be, but if that was her intention why not just bring the king's men with her?" Zollie placed his hand on Akim's shoulder and whispered in his ear. "I suppose we don't have much choice, my brother, but to trust her. If Jehovah wants to spare us, then He may have brought this woman to lead us to safety."

By now the woman was showing her impatience and fear. "If you don't come now, we may never make it to my house without the guards seeing us. You must trust me." Without another word, the woman turned and headed down the rock road. The men followed after her. By now the shadows of evening were settling in and people were closing up their shops to head home. Several shop owners gave the two men probing stares as they followed behind the woman. A large group of soldiers came running toward them. The woman stopped abruptly, grabbed Akim by the arm and pulled him toward her. She put her arms around his neck and pretended to be talking with him. Zollie followed suit and turned his back to the road. The group of men glanced at the threesome and then hurried on.

"Quickly, it's not far now. If we can make it a few more blocks….just a few more blocks." The woman was breathing heavily and urged the two men to move faster. "Here...here it is." The woman hastily opened a wooden door and closed it with a bang as Zollie and Akim crossed the threshold. She threw her veil from her head as she began climbing the outside stone stair case toward the roof top. "I'll hide you up here."

Reaching the roof, Akim and Zollie's eyes met neat rows of flax lying on the roof top floor to dry. "You want us to hide here?" Zollie asked in a surprised voice.

"Yes, quickly cover yourself with the flax." As she finished her instructions, a determined knock at her door caused her to turn abruptly and head back down the stairs. "I'll be back for you later." Her voice echoed in the stair way. The two men wasted no time in covering themselves with the stalks. They listened and could pick up men's voices coming from downstairs. The woman's voice could be heard from time to time. It seemed an eternity before the woman made her way back upstairs carrying an oil lamp to light her way. She placed the lamp on the ledge of the roof top.

"You can come out now; you're safe. I told them that you had been here, but you left the city in the darkness. I said for them to pursue you on the road leading to the Jordan and they might be able to catch you. They believed my story and won't be back for some time. They'll assume you escaped."

"What made them think to look for us in your house?" Akim asked in a suspicious tone.

The woman lowered her head then looked back at Akim. "Most every visitor to Jericho comes to my house....sooner or later." Her voice emanated emotion. "I'm well known in the city and easy to find."

Akim continued to study the woman in the dim light of the oil lamp. She was young—maybe twenty-three and she had stunning raven black hair. Her facial features were graceful but Akim could see sadness in her dark eyes. *She's a harlot*, Akim thought to himself. *A harlot has brought us into her house.*

***

As we move into the book of Joshua, we find that it's now time for the Hebrew children to enter and possess the land God has promised Abraham many years earlier. Moses was dead and Joshua was now the military leader of the Hebrews. He sent two spies to cross the Jordan River, find out all they could, and report back as quickly as possible. The spies entered Jericho as instructed and were soon in danger from the king's men. Everyone in the land of Canaan heard about how God had supernaturally brought millions of Hebrews out of their bondage in Egypt and how they had defeated the Amorites. Now they were on the move, and immense fear had gripped the people living in Canaan. The power of Jehovah God was more than they could fathom.

Although we may wrestle with the fact that God had commanded the Hebrews to kill everyone in the new land they would inherit, nevertheless, He did. I think if we could understand how evil this society had become we might have a better understanding. But the fact that Rahab and all her family was saved shows that God still held out his hand to anyone willing to believe. In fact, Rahab is listed in the "hall of faith" recorded in the book of Hebrews 11:30-31.

Rahab had listened to all the stories regarding the God of the Hebrews and she reasoned that none of her gods had ever been able to perform such magnificent miracles. Although the other peoples of the land were also frightened, Rahab acted upon that fear and made the choice to follow the Hebrew God. She sided with the two spies against her own people. Putting her life in danger, she hid them and then helped them to escape. She knew that within days the Hebrews would cross the Jordan and attack her city. She reasoned that the great wall around the city would offer little challenge to a God who had parted the Red Sea.

The account of Rahab in the Old Testament should give us encouragement that even a heathen girl raised from birth in an idol worshiping nation, living a life of utter sinfulness can be transformed by the supernatural working of a sovereign God. Even in this dark, remote, and evil society, God's hand can and does penetrate hearts. When the two spies arrived in Jericho, God had already moved in the life of this woman. Not only did Rahab rescue herself, but she rescued her entire family. No one—regardless of the circumstance—is beyond the saving grace of God. What a marvelous Redeemer!

Will the Real Mother Please Stand Up?

> "Then two women who were harlots came to the king and stood before him" (1 Kings 3:16).

The tiny baby boy squirmed as he lay on the floor in front of the two women. He grabbed his foot and began playing with his toes. His cooing filtered throughout the throne room of King Solomon.

The king sat silent looking at both women as they told their differing stories. They both claimed to be the mother of this infant and each of them presented a scenario that could not be proven. There had been no witnesses to confirm or disprove either one.

One of the palace guards leaned toward his companion and whispered, "These are only harlots. Why would the king take the time to listen to their silly pleas? Besides, there is no way to determine which one is telling the truth."

"But my Lord," continued the first woman, "this is my child—this woman is lying when she says it is her child."

"Oh, no, I'm not. The dead child is yours. This child is mine." insisted the other.

King Solomon breathed a heavy sigh. "This is a difficult case since no witnesses were present to confirm either story." Solomon turned to a guard standing close by. "Draw your sword and come here."

Come, Let Us Reason Together

There was a hush over the crowd gathered to see how the king would handle this case. After all, Solomon had been given wisdom by God above anyone who had ever lived. People from everywhere came to hear his insight on any subject known. But this case would be a challenge and the people of Jerusalem were curious to see how he would judge.

Solomon's tone was harsh. "Cut the baby in half and give part to one of the women and the other part to the other woman."

The first woman smirked. "Yes, yes, that's the fair thing to do. Kill the baby so that neither of us can have him."

The other fell on her knees and gave out a gasp. She held out her hands in a praying position. "No, my Lord, no! Please have mercy. She can have the child. I'll do anything you wish, but please do not harm the baby." Tears began to flow down her cheeks and onto the floor.

Solomon rose from his throne and walked in front of the kneeling harlot. He reached down and gently pulled her to her feet. "Give the baby to this woman. She is the mother and he is her child."

***

This seems to be a strange account, but we are told that the people who witnessed this saw that King Solomon had truly been given wisdom by God and that his ruling in this case was just. Justice is a sweet word and we all long for it. We don't see much accurate justice today. It seems the wicked go free while the innocent die.

It would be nice to have leaders with wisdom to do the just thing. In Scripture we are told that, "The fear of the Lord is the beginning of wisdom" (Psalms 111:10a). Only in God can man find true wisdom. Someday there will be justice, and it will be ministered by someone greater than Solomon.

In Hebrews 9:27 we are told that "it is appointed for man to die once and after this comes judgment." Just like the true mother in our story, we better be sure we are true believers. The following verse in our Hebrews passage goes on to say, "So Christ also, having been offered once to bear the sins of many, will appear a second time for salvation without reference to sin, to those who eagerly await Him." Will the true believers please stand up!

Hang On, Saints

"For I consider that the sufferings of this present time are not worthy to be compared with the glory that is to be revealed to us" (Romans 8:18).

We live in an age of instant gratification. I'm old enough to remember when it took over an hour to bake a potato, you had to actually go to the bank to deposit money, and a mailed written check would sometimes take ten days to clear your account. I must admit I rather liked that because it gave me time to deposit enough money to cover my obligation. People were more patient years ago because they had no choice about it.

I'd like to think I'm a forbearing person, but one test you can use to determine how forbearing you are is in the area of trials. I lay my problems before God and actually expect an instantaneous solution. What is really telling about yourself is your anger with God for not meeting your time table and expectations. Ever do that? I have many times.

If you do a word study on the word "wait" in Scripture, you'll be shocked at the many times we are told to wait on the Lord. You see, God is not in a rush. He doesn't work from the standpoint of time. He works from the standpoint of eternity.

Psalms 37:7 tells us to wait patiently for the Lord because in due time our enemies will be defeated; in Proverbs 20:22 we are told not to form our own vigilante campaign but to wait for God to punish evil; in Isaiah 40:31 we are promised that those who wait on the Lord will be given strength beyond their ability; and in Isaiah 64:4 we are told that God will act in behalf of those who wait for Him.

The area of waiting that means the most to me is in regard to our final redemption. If you read Romans 8:18-25 you learn that believers are told to wait patiently for that day when the curse of Genesis 3 will be reversed. Not only was man subjected to the curse of sin, but the creation was as well. In fact, it seems that creation knows the severity of the curse better than man does. In Romans 8:20-21, it says that the whole of creation is in a state of anxious waiting and groaning for the revealing of the sons of God. The creation must wait for our redemption before it will be set free. The Apostle Paul had that kind of excitement. He was eagerly waiting for our Lord's return and our adoption as sons, which is the redemption of our body. You'll have to admit that most believers don't show that kind of passion to be set free. Most of us have come to love the trinkets of life on earth above that of being with our Lord.

For a Christian, this world is only temporary. Someday it will be destroyed. We are but sojourners waiting for the time when either God calls us home or Jesus keeps the promise to His disciples and to us that He will return. Are we eagerly waiting that time? Are we waiting patiently until He comes?

"Wait for the Lord; be strong, and let your heart take courage; yes, wait for the Lord" (Psalms 27:14).

A Dirty Word

"Blessed is the man whom You chasten, O Lord, and whom You teach out of Your law" (Psalms 94:12).

Discipline—what a dirty word. Some would say I need to wash my mouth out with soap. That word is offensive to many people and considered a brutal concept. We live in a day of unruly passions. We're told that whatever a person does—as long as it doesn't hurt anyone else—is OK and no one has the right to say it's wrong. It's called relativism.

I don't think God received the memo about the change. He still operates as usual and He still considers some things sinful and unacceptable. There are several words used for the concept of discipline in the Bible: chasten, reprove, and correct are just a few.

God believes so strongly in correcting His people that in Proverbs 3:11-12 we are told that the fact that the Lord disciplines us proves that He loves us. That same concept is repeated in the New Testament in Hebrews 12:5-6.

You don't read deep into Genesis before you see man requiring the discipline of God; in fact, it's in the first three chapters. From the time of the fall, man has been fighting against the laws and character of his Creator, and so God has extended His hand of authority and power over man's rebellious actions.

Through the Mosaic law, God revealed His righteous principles. The Hebrew people were to act differently from the nations around them. They were to reflect the holiness of their God. Because God knew that they could never meet those standards, He gave them animal sacrifices as a temporary atonement. A greater provision would be made at a future point in history. But even in this temporary provision, He gave the Hebrews disciplinary practices in order to remind the people that certain behavior would not be tolerated. We are often astonished that many of these sins demanded a death penalty. And, if the people failed to exert discipline, God would.

As we move into the New Testament, we understand that Jesus the Christ is that permanent atonement. God began to work through the church as His ambassador to the world and to show forth His holiness and grace. He gave the Holy Spirit to those who embraced His Son in order to give them the ability to walk honorably before their God and before mankind. Perhaps the last bastion of authority is the church. It may come as a surprise to some church goers that our Lord gave specific instructions for church discipline, because the rebelliousness exhibited by our forefathers is still active and alive within the church family. Discipline is still as needed today as it was in the Old Testament economy. And although the punishment demanded under the law of Moses is not the same for us today, we make a mistake if we think God has changed His mind about certain behavior.

Our Lord knew that shortly after He ascended back to the Father, the church would be born. While still on earth, Jesus taught His disciples some guiding principles for bringing a church member into discipline. We find these guidelines recorded in Matthew 18:15-17, and they offer a step by step process that should be followed. Although there is not a detailed outline for this process, it gives us a good start toward handling believers who have ventured into persistent sinful behavior.

Perhaps the strongest example of church discipline is given in Acts 5:1-11, and it is actually carried out supernaturally. Two of the early church members were not truthful in telling the apostles about a gift they had given. In order to show how God feels about lying, these two people were instantly put to death by God. Not all believers who lie are instantly put to death, but the point is clear that the church is held to a higher standard.

It's important that we don't confuse discipline with punishment. True discipline is designed to bring an erring brother back into right standing before God and the church. In 2 Thessalonians 3:14-15, we are told that if a brother does not obey the commands of Christ we are to put him to shame by not associating with him. But, we are not to consider him an enemy, but as a brother in Christ.

There is a warning to be watchful that while we are admonishing others, we ourselves don't fall into similar sin. All these instructions are designed to maintain a healthy church body, and to make sure our Lord is not held up to ridicule because of us.

It is much better if we discipline ourselves. There's an interesting statement in 1 Corinthians 11:31 that says, "If we judged ourselves rightly, we would not be judged." Although the context of that verse has reference to the Lord's Table and making sure we do not lightly esteem that church ordinance, I think it can have practical application to everyday life. The instant we know that sin has entered our thinking or our actions, we can immediately go before our Lord and ask His forgiveness. He has promised to be faithful and forgive us. Much embarrassment, hurt, and tears could be avoided by simply conducting self-discipline.

Not many of our churches practice church discipline today. In fact, some churches have been sued by those who have been disciplined. Our secular society has convinced most denominations that no one has the right to judge someone else. They tell us that we all sin and therefore to bring discipline upon someone else is hypocritical. It's no wonder that within our churches we tolerate every kind of sinful behavior. The outside world looks at those who call themselves followers of Christ and sees no difference between our lifestyle and their own. It brings ridicule and shame to us, and it doesn't glorify our Lord.

Muddy River

"Now Naaman, captain of the army of the king of Aram, was a great man with his master, and highly respected, because by him the Lord had given victory to Aram. The man was also a valiant warrior, but he was a leper" (2 Kings 5:1).

I lived most of my life in Oklahoma and in my small community the Washita River bordered one side of our town and Rush Creek the other. During heavy rains, both would flood and you could paddle your boat down Main Street. As a kid, my sister and I would wade in the water that lapped up over our front porch, but then our parents would take us to the doctor for the dreaded tetanus shot because the water was filthy. That river and the creek were always muddy and a sickening brownish color. The only good thing about either one was fishing for cat fish—or you could go noodling—but that's another story.

The story in 2 Kings 5:1-14 is the narrative of another muddy river. It's the story of a military captain named Naaman from the ancient country of Aram located near Damascus in Syria. He was a favorite of the King of Aram because he was so successful in his military campaigns. In fact, we are told something that probably Naaman didn't even know—it was the Lord God of Israel who had given this captain his victories. But Naaman had a big problem. He was a leper.

Leprosy was a hideous disease in Old Testament times. There were many forms of the disease, but all of the various types caused extreme deformities to the body and were incurable.

During one of Naaman's military endeavors, he raided a village in Israel and took a young girl as a slave to attend his wife. We don't know how old she was at the time of her abduction, but she was old enough to remember a great Jewish prophet living in Israel near Samaria named Elisha. More than likely, Naaman had killed her parents and perhaps all her family. That was the Syrian way. But he had spared the little girl—not because he had compassion for her, but to serve his family. And even if Naaman had not killed her family, he had taken her away from her homeland and she was a slave. The fact that the little girl showed Naaman compassion is very interesting.

The name of the little Jewish girl is not given, but she was used by God to save this Syrian military man and to show forth the mercy of God even toward those who do not acknowledge Him. We call it common grace. We have that spelled out for us in Matthew 5:44-45 by the Lord Himself.

In our story about Naaman we have a little girl who shows us the way we are to treat those outside the faith. Please don't misunderstand. Those outside the faith are still lost, and there are times we must stand up to evil and admonish those who practice wickedness, but when possible, we are to show mercy to those who are our enemies.

Our little heroine remembered the Jewish prophet in Samaria and told her mistress that he could heal her husband of leprosy. Naaman received permission to travel to Israel to seek the help of the holy man, but Naaman first journeyed to the king of Israel's palace. The king of Israel thought Naaman was looking for an excuse to invade his land and went into a panic. It's sad that the king of Israel had no confidence either in God or in God's prophet to heal this man. A captured slave girl exhibited more faith than he did.

When Elisha hears about the king's dilemma, he sends word to have Naaman come to his house. Elisha writes to the king that he will heal Naaman, and then everyone will know there is a prophet in Israel.

I can visualize this next scene. Naaman comes riding to the home of Elisha in his chariot with his spirited battle horses along with military men in their chariots at his side. They would have worn clothing of bright colors symbolizing their importance. Naaman was not in the habit of visiting such unimportant men as Elisha and begging for their help. It went against his narcissistic personality. Before Naaman dismounted his chariot, a messenger from Elisha approached him. "My master has sent me to tell you to wash in the Jordan River seven times and your flesh will be restored to you and you will be clean."

Naaman was furious. He already had in mind how Elisha would heal him. He thought Elisha would perform some type of spiritual ritual, but to wash in the muddy Jordan River was beneath him. Why not send him back to the clean waters of Syria? Would that not have been better for a man of his standing? In total disgust, Naaman mounted his chariot and rode back toward his home.

I must say that this man Naaman was truly blessed. Several of his servants pled with him to give it a try since they were already close to the Jordan. They reasoned that if Elisha had told him to do some great feat, he would have certainly done that, so why not try the muddy river? So he did. Six times he washed and nothing happened. Then on the seventh time, when he arose from the water, he was clean as a new born baby!

Isn't it interesting that men think they have a better idea of how to be saved by God than God does? Some say we must do certain works before God will save us while others believe if we perform particular rituals we will gain favor from God. Others say no matter how hard we try, we can never really be sure of obtaining God's forgiveness. Just like Naaman, we want to come up with our own idea of deliverance. But Naaman was forced to follow Elisha's instructions if healing was to take place. And likewise God says eternal deliverance must be His way. We make it hard; God makes it simple. "Believe in the Lord Jesus, and you shall be saved" (Acts 16:31).

A Supercilious Woman

"Now it was told King David, saying, 'The Lord has blessed the house of Obed-edom and all that belongs to him, on account of the ark of God.' David went and brought up the ark of God from the house of Obed-edom into the city of David with gladness" (2 Samuel 6:12).

God selected David to replace Saul as king in Israel. It had been a long, arduous road for David. Month upon month of running, hiding, and trying to stay alive as Saul relentlessly pursued him over harsh mountain terrain. Now he was king and his desire was to bring the ark of the covenant to the newly declared capital of Israel—Jerusalem. The temple was not yet built so the ark was to be housed in a tent. When all was ready, David traveled to the house of Obed-edom and fetched the ark. As they approached the city, David set aside his royal robes and clothed himself with a linen ephod. The linen ephod was normally worn by the priests, and although David was not a priest, he humbled himself to wear a symbol of those who served before God.

David was so joyous in bringing the ark to Jerusalem that he danced unashamedly as the procession moved toward the city. The ark of the covenant was the meeting place between God and man. It was housed in the Holy of Holies and once each year the high priest sprinkled blood upon the ark and secured forgiveness from God for the Jewish people. For David, this was a glorious beginning of Israel as a united kingdom under the blessings of Jehovah God. David's intention was to build a magnificent temple patterned after the tabernacle in the wilderness, but that would have to wait until David's son, Solomon, was king.

The whole city was exuberant and proud of that day—well, not the whole city. There was one woman watching from her window at the sight taking place below her who was bitter and vengeful in her heart. Her name was Michal and she was the wife of David. Her father was Saul, who had formally been the king. Saul had given Michal to David as a wife, but when he learned David was to replace him on the throne, he was jealous and became determined to kill David. David had to flee Jerusalem. In an act of hateful indignation, Saul gave Michal to another man as his wife. When Saul was dead, David sent for his wife, Michal. That's a sad story you can read about in 2 Samuel 3:14-16.

Michal could have been bitter over David's ascending to her father's throne, or she could have been bitter over having to leave her second husband. My personal feeling is that Michal was ashamed because in her eyes David had lowered himself to the common man by removing his royal garments and dancing in front of the ark. Pride or bitterness will eventually cause you to make a fatal misstep. God had ordained David as king and Michal was his wife. David would be judged for his sins, but this was not one of them. His happiness and humility in bringing the Mosaic ark of the covenant to Jerusalem was sanctioned by God, and when Michal belittled David's worship, she stepped over the line. God made Michal barren.

I often think of the unbelieving world as they poke fun and belittle those who love the Lord. We are humiliated in the

Come, Let Us Reason Together

public square and fair game for comedians. The early church suffered more than just humiliation—they were imprisoned or killed. The Apostle Paul tells his student, Timothy, "Therefore do not be ashamed of the testimony of our Lord or of me His prisoner, but join with me in suffering for the gospel according to the power of God" (2 Timothy 1:8). Are we unashamed to proclaim Christ, or does our pride and the prospect of ridicule keep us silent?

A Profitable Death

"I have been crucified with Christ; and it is no longer I who live, but Christ lives in me" (Galatians 2:20a).

The word "death" always conjures up negative feelings. It has the idea of finality. No one enjoys attending funerals, but sometimes we must. In fact, our modern culture is so obsessed with minimizing death that we've come up with other ways to express that reality. We use words such as expire, pass away, demise or deceased.

The Apostle Paul was proud of his death, because his death brought true life. He's speaking spiritually of course, but the death he speaks about is just as real as any physical death. He goes on to say in Galatians 2:20b, "And the life which I now live in the flesh I live by faith in the Son of God, who loved me, and gave Himself up for me."

In order to understand more about the death Paul was proud to proclaim, look at Romans 6:6: "Knowing this, that our old self was crucified with Him, in order that our body of sin might be done away with, so that we would no longer be slaves to sin." Here we learn it's our old sin nature that has died, and we've been released from the bondage of sin. We'll sin as believers, but now we have an option. You are to "consider yourselves to be dead to sin, but alive to God in Christ Jesus" (Romans 6:11). It's a mental thought process whereby we understand that when Christ died on that Roman cross, we died with Him, and when Christ was raised, we were raised up with Him to newness of life. We no longer need to be a slave to sin.

Paul reminded us in his letter to the church at Galatia that, "It was for freedom that Christ set us free; therefore keep standing firm and do not be subject again to a yoke of slavery" (Galatians 5:1). As a believer, we can choose to live our lives unshackled by sin, or we can chain ourselves back to that lifestyle. You now have a choice. Going to the funeral of our old sinful nature is one funeral we should be proud to attend.

Disqualified

> "But I discipline my body and make it my slave, so that, after I have preached to others, I myself will not be disqualified" (1 Corinthians 9:27).

Perhaps the most terrifying word an athlete can hear is disqualified. I think that's why Paul used that analogy in his letter to the Corinthians. Being from Oklahoma, I grew up learning about an Oklahoma native they called the greatest athlete who ever lived, Jim Thorpe. He was proficient at any sport he tried—track, football, baseball, and basketball. In 1912, he won Olympic gold medals for pentathlon and decathlon. Six months after the games, it was discovered that Thorpe had played for a minor league baseball club. It was ruled that technically that made him a professional and therefore he could not participate in the Olympic Games. He was disqualified and the medals were withdrawn. Jim Thorpe was depressed and devastated. Thirty years after his death, the International Olympic Committee restored his Olympic medals, but he was not there to enjoy the victory.

We live our Christian lives knowing that we are easily tempted by sin. I'm sure you know, as I do, the names of once prominent Christian leaders who became entangled in unscriptural behavior and not only lost their position, but lost their influence and reputations. We can also see some great men of the Old Testament who wavered and fell into disqualifying sin. David was the greatest king of Israel, and yet he committed adultery with a married woman while her husband was away fighting for Israel. Solomon, who was given wisdom by God above anyone who ever lived, ended his life in total despair crying "vanity, vanity, all is vanity."

We sometime put the early apostles on a pedestal and think they had no problems with sin. Paul was well aware of his frailties and he kept himself disciplined. He feared after teaching God's Word to others, he himself would become disqualified. Paul knew nothing would separate him from Christ (Romans 8:38-39), but he knew he could lose his influence with others. The key to staying on track, Paul tells us, is self-control. He compares the Christian walk to an athlete who constantly trains to stay in shape.

During the summer Olympics, I love hearing the commentators give information regarding the various athletes. Most of them don't have a normal life. They train for hours each day; they watch what food they eat; and they have no time for personal relationships which might become a hindrance to their goal of winning a medal. I have to admire their tenacity and determination.

Believers in Jesus Christ are training too. Our prize will not be an earthly one, but a heavenly one. It takes as much dedication and commitment to be a Christian as any athlete who ever lived. Our routines are a little different from an athlete's. They use weight machines, endurance drills, diets, and running. We use the Bible, prayer, and fellowship with other believers. There are days that an athlete dreads his workout, but if he's determined, he'll do them anyway. We too, as Christians, sometimes don't want to bother with our spiritual exercises, but if we're resolute, we'll persevere.

Bloodline

"And to Obed was born Jesse, and to Jesse, David"
(Ruth 4:22).

The old woman held the baby boy close as she sang a Jewish hymn. Her face glowed with pride and happiness. As Obed slept peacefully against her, Naomi thought back over the past few years. *How long had it been?* Naomi tried to remember when her husband had loaded up their two sons, Mahlon and Chilion, and left their land and most of their possessions in Israel to move to the land of Moab just south of Bethlehem. A famine had plagued their land unmercifully for many months and her husband, Elimelech, had made the decision to leave Judah and find work elsewhere.

It had been a hard journey, not to mention leaving family, but Naomi felt she must follow her husband. Moab had not been friendly toward Jews, and the Moabite religious beliefs were of idols and myths, but they had made their place among the Gentiles, and raised the two boys in a foreign land.

Naomi's eyes filled with tears as she remembered her husband's death, but she had felt safe knowing her two sons were close by. They had married Moabite women of good quality, if not of the same religious background as their Jewish husbands. But then Naomi knew her family had not kept active in their Jewish customs.

Come, Let Us Reason Together

A tear fell on the baby's arm and Naomi quickly wiped it off. She tried to forget the next tragedy of her life in Moab, but nothing could block the memory from her mind. Shortly after the death of her husband, the unthinkable happened. Both sons also died and worse still, they had left no heirs to carry on the family name.

The decision to leave Moab and return to Bethlehem had not been easy, but Naomi knew she had to go back to her own country. She was an older woman and wasn't sure she could make it home by herself—bandits, wild animals, and the long walk would probably take her first. None of that mattered to her; death seemed a pleasant release from her tragedies.

A smile emerged on Naomi's lips as she remembered the loyalty and love both daughter-in-laws had shown her. Both wanted to go with her, but Naomi knew that would be a disastrous decision. There were so many negatives—differences in religion, economic problems, future husbands for them in a hostile environment, and the biggest problem of all—God had turned his back on Naomi. But in spite of all that, one of her daughter-in-laws would not listen. Ruth refused to turn away and even swore to embrace Naomi's God as her own. The two women had returned alone to Bethlehem. They had no land; they had no man to protect and provide for them; and the people were cautious of a Moabite woman. Naomi was so distressed that she told her neighbors to rename her Bitter.

The thought of that made Naomi laugh out loud. What a fool she'd been. How faithless. Far from abandoning her, God had a magnificent plan for Ruth and Naomi. Now she sat in a fine house with servants, all the food she wanted, protected as never before, and holding a child that would be as one of her own.

Obed awakened and interrupted Naomi's thoughts. She picked him up and wrapped her arms around his small body. *I wonder who you will be*, she thought. *Perhaps a great king or savior of Israel. If only I could look into the future. But I know God has something special planned for you, my little Obed. After all, Jehovah God is faithful.*

***

If you've read the book of Ruth, you know the working of God in the lives of these two women. And, if you read Matthew 1:5 you know that Obed is in the bloodline of our Lord and Savior, Jesus Christ. It seems strange that God would select a Gentile woman from Moab to be the great-grandmother of King David, whose line eventually continues on to the birth of our Lord! God told Abraham that through him all the world would be blessed. Not only the Jews would enjoy the blessings of Abraham, but the Gentiles would also enjoy them. I think the story of Ruth is a glimpse into that fulfillment. In the book of Acts, we see that come to fruition through the founding of the church where both Jew and Gentile are invited to join.

It is God who takes center stage in the story of Ruth. Elimelech and Naomi lost faith in God's provision and went into a Gentile land; because of that, their two sons married Gentile women, which was forbidden in Jewish law. Naomi even changed her name to reflect her lack of faith in Jehovah; even through all that, God worked to bring blessing to Naomi and the fulfillment of His eternal plan. What a God we worship!

Do You Have Humility?

"Do nothing from selfishness or empty conceit, but with humility of mind regard one another as more important than yourselves" (Philippians 2:3).

If you answered "yes," then you don't have it, but if you answered "I don't know," then there may be some hope that you do. Humility is one of those elusive traits that only God can discern in our hearts for sure. The second you consider yourself humble, it vanishes, and even if you're doing unselfish looking things, it may come from a wrong motive. As with most righteous attributes, humility starts with a certain mindset.

When we look at Paul's instructions to the church at Philippi in Philippians 2:3, we think, *Paul, you've got to be kidding. I might be able to put my family ahead of myself, but others? You don't know some of the people in my church or my neighbors.* Paul goes on to say we are to place the interest of others ahead of our own.

Why can Paul ask such a seemingly impossible thing? We find out in the verses that follow. Christ Jesus, the one who created everything, who occupied heaven and had equality with God the Father, came to earth as a baby taking on the form of man. He laid aside His royalty for the dregs of humanity. Then He submitted himself to death on a Roman cross. I will never be able to fully grasp or understand that. But I can show my appreciation by exhibiting unselfish love. Every time I place someone's interest ahead of mine, or love someone who is unlovable, I exhibit Christ.

These are hard lessons to learn because we live in a "me" generation. We look to others to fulfill our needs and interests. We're very protective of our rights and we don't like someone getting the better of us. I'm so grateful that our Lord and Savior didn't behave as we do and was willing to humble Himself on our behalf. The world considers humble people weak. What do you think? It's a lot harder to act in a humble manner than to look after number one. After all, looking out for number one comes naturally to us and takes absolutely no effort.

Our Honored Guest

"Do you not know that you are a temple of God and that the Spirit of God dwells in you? If any man destroys the temple of God, God will destroy him, for the temple of God is holy, and that is what you are" (1 Corinthians 3:16-17).

While Jesus was walking and teaching in Israel, He made some interesting statements about the Holy Spirit. The disciples didn't really understand at the time what the ramifications of those statements would mean in their lives, but they soon would. If you've studied the Old Testament, you know that many times the Holy Spirit helped God's people accomplish a difficult task. Probably one of the best known is Samson. His story is found in Judges 13 through 16. Samson is a bittersweet story of a man who was used by God in spite of Samson's erratic behavior.

The Philistines were invading villages of Israel and causing all kinds of problems. God called Samson to fight against the Philistines and save his people. To do that, God gave him strength beyond any man, and Samson was able to inflict some heavy blows to the enemy. Although he didn't know it, his strength came from the Holy Spirit. He actually thought it was from his long, black, curly locks.

Samson became involved with a heathen woman which was against Jewish law. They had an illicit love affair and the woman was able to turn Samson over to the Philistines.

Mary Baird

Perhaps one of the saddest statements in the Old Testament is in Judges 16:20b, "But he did not know that the Lord had departed from him." Samson lost all his strength in a split second because God removed the Holy Spirit from him. In Old Testament days, the Holy Spirit would come and go from people as needed. The Holy Spirit was not a permanent guest.

That's what makes the teachings of Jesus regarding the Holy Spirit so wonderful. The night our Lord was betrayed, He told His disciples as recorded in John 14:16, "I will ask the Father, and He will give you another Helper [the Holy Spirit], that He may be with you forever." As you read the rest of that section, you learn how important the Holy Spirit is in the life of a believer. On this side of the cross, the Holy Spirit indwells us and will never leave us. He is our guarantee to heaven (Ephesians 4:30); He teaches us truth (John 14:26); He gives us spiritual gifts (1 Corinthians 12:1-11); He takes our prayers and delivers them to God perfectly (Romans 8:26); and much, much more.

Paul makes an interesting point in his first letter to the church at Corinth. He says in 1 Corinthians 3:16-17, that because the Holy Spirit indwells us, we are considered temples of God. No wonder we are admonished to live our lives in purity (1 Corinthians 6:19-20). Jesus told His disciples that He would not leave them orphans. Even though He must leave them, Jesus would send them the Holy Spirit. As believers in Jesus Christ, we have that same promise. The Holy Spirit is truly our honored guest.

Torn Curtain

"And Jesus cried out again with a loud voice, and yielded up His spirit. And behold, the veil of the temple was torn in two from top to bottom; and the earth shook and the rocks were split" (Matthew 27:50-51).

When God gave Moses the detailed plans for the tabernacle in the wilderness as recorded in Exodus, it had three main areas. Outside was the court where the sacrifices were offered; inside the tent was the Holy Place where the priests ministered before the table of showbread, the table of incense, and the golden lamp stand. A thick tapestry curtain was placed at the back of the Holy Place. The room behind that curtain was called the Holy of Holies. No one could go into that room except the High Priest and only once a year. Inside the Holy of Holies was the ark of the covenant or mercy seat. The curtain was made to show that man was not able to come before a holy God. In fact, the High Priest who went in each year may have tied a rope around his ankle in case God became angry for some reason and they died. He could be pulled out by the rope since no one would dare enter and bring him out.

Unless you're Jewish or have studied the tabernacle, the furnishings are probably not familiar to you. The important thing to know is that in instructing the placement of the curtain in front of the Holy of Holies, the Jews were to understand that because of sin, man and God could not fellowship without a representative. In the Old Testament, that representative was the high priest. For hundreds of years, the high priest was the only man who could go inside that curtain on the Day of Atonement. He would take some blood from an animal sacrifice and sprinkle it on the ark of the covenant. In performing this act, the High Priest was asking God to forgive the sins of the Jewish people and allow them to live one more year.

God showed the Jews that all those sacrifices they offered were evidence that sins could never be forgiven without the shedding of blood (Hebrews 9:22). Then we find out that the blood of bulls and goats could never really cover sin (Hebrews 10:4). So what was man to do? Was he stuck in his sin forever without any remedy? God had the perfect plan. His Son would come to earth, be conceived by a virgin into the human race without the problem of sin inherited by a human father, and assume the role of a sinless sacrifice. He would shed His blood as the payment that God demanded.

To demonstrate to man that the sacrifice made by Jesus Christ was sufficient and acceptable, God tore the curtain in the temple from top to bottom just as a woman rips an old piece of cloth. At the exact time our Lord gave up His Spirit, the thick tapestry curtain was no longer needed. What a beautiful picture of God's approval. Today the way to God is open to mankind through the sacrifice of Christ, and man can fellowship with God anytime and anywhere without needing any man to act as an intermediary. Believers are allowed to enter into the Holy of Holies because the blood of Christ has been sprinkled on the mercy seat once and for all.

Intelligent Love

"And this I pray, that your love may abound still more and more in real knowledge and all discernment" (Philippians 1:9).

The word "love" is a word we throw around rather randomly. From our pets to our favorite food, we use the word to describe the pleasure we derive from these things. Because we have a varied use of the word, there has been disillusionment on the part of some who have been told they are "loved" to then find out the person making that statement meant something entirely different. We fall in and out of love much as a child discards one toy and is ready for something new.

How are we to know true love from that which is, at best, shallow and momentary, and at worst, deceitful? Marriages are falling apart because two people who had pledged to love and cherish one another until death now say they have "fallen out of love" with their partner.

The best place to begin our search for genuine love is with the One whose very nature is love (1 John 4:16). God created the universe with hundreds of galaxies but chose to place His particular attention on the planet we call Earth, and focus His love on those who reside there. We are told that "God so loved the world, that He gave His only begotten Son, that whoever believes in Him shall not perish, but have eternal life" (John 3:16). Since God is entirely holy and cannot sin, then His love is perfect. We can come to an understanding of ideal love by looking into God's Word.

The Apostle Paul wrote a letter to the church that met in Philippi in order to encourage them in their convictions and remind them to remain faithful. Paul tells them, "And this I pray, that your love may abound still more and more in real knowledge and all discernment, so that you may approve the things that are excellent, in order to be sincere and blameless until the day of Christ" (Philippians 1:9-10).

We sometimes think of love as strictly an emotion. We either feel love for someone or we don't. How often have you heard the words "I just don't feel anything for them"? According to our verse in Philippians, love is much more than an emotion. Notice that Paul does not say that he prayed that their love would abound more and more in real feeling, but in real knowledge. Knowledge has substance. Knowledge is based on our knowing certain things we've learned and knowledge is not dependent on how we feel. I must abide by the law of gravity whether I feel like it or not. And so I can love someone regardless of my feelings. Feelings may or may not follow.

Two words that Paul used to describe love are knowledge and discernment; your translation may have the words stated differently, but they mean the same thing. We should ask: knowledge about what and discernment about what? We could spend weeks on just these two words, but we'll just highlight.

Knowledge as related to love means knowing what is expected of us. Have you ever done a word study on 1 Corinthians 13:4-13? It's sobering when we understand the depth of commitment required by God if we are to love intelligently.

Come, Let Us Reason Together

Discernment, as related to love, refers to the ability to size up a person in order to act in their best interest. Sometimes that means tough love and discipline, and sometimes that means endurance and grace.

We won't always get it right in our ability to love as God does. The more we understand the divine love God has lavished on us, the easier it is for us to love that same way. It means dying to ourselves and preferring others. That's not our natural instinct—especially in today's culture with its "me first!" mentality—but the rewards of selfless love are endless.

When the Saints Go Marching In

> "Paul, called as an apostle of Jesus Christ by the will of God, and Sosthenes our brother, to the church of God which is at Corinth, to those who have been sanctified in Christ Jesus, saints by calling, with all who in every place call upon the name of our Lord Jesus Christ, their Lord and ours" (1 Corinthians 1:1-2).

Have you ever called anyone a "saint"? Usually it's someone you admire or has done extra special things in your life or the lives of others. Some interpret that word to mean a person of high character who has been canonized as a saint. The Greek word as used in the New Testament actually means "most holy thing."[2]

None of us would categorize ourselves as a saint, but if you are a believer in Jesus Christ and have accepted Him as your Savior, that's exactly what you are! In the Apostle Paul's letter to the church at Corinth, he calls them saints. Notice the criteria he uses to dub them by that word. He says, "to those who have been sanctified in Christ Jesus, saints by calling, with all who in every place call on the name of our Lord Jesus Christ, their Lord and ours." Paul says being a saint means you have named Jesus as your Lord and Savior. God has allowed

---

2. Blue Letter Bible. "Dictionary and Word Search for hagios (Strong's 40)". Blue Letter Bible. 1996-2012. 20 Dec 2012. < http:// www.blueletterbible.org/lang/lexicon/lexicon.cfm?Strongs=G40&t=KJV >

you the distinction of being declared most holy and set apart because you have assumed the righteousness of Christ.

The letter to the Corinthians is not the only letter where Paul refers to the believers as saints. In Ephesians 1:1, he uses the same description for them. He says, "To the saints who are at Ephesus and who are faithful in Christ Jesus."

Makes you feel rather special, doesn't it? The problem is that those who are in Christ don't always act like saints. In fact, we can act every bit as badly as those who know nothing about the Lord. When Paul wrote his letter to the Corinthians, he was extremely displeased with their behavior and spent most of the letter correcting them. Some were living in sin, some were causing divisions in the church, and some were conducting the Lord's Supper in a displeasing manner. And yet, Paul could refer to them as saints.

Man adds more to the meaning of the word "saint." You must be an extraordinary person who has done extraordinary service to have that title—like a Mother Teresa or some philanthropic person. But the Bible has a different meaning of the word. According to the Bible usage, you cannot do anything good enough to be called a saint. Only by receiving Christ as your Savior can you be given that lofty name. There have been many people canonized as saints who weren't saints—much like the catchy phrase, "There's a lot of people talkin' 'bout heaven who ain't goin' there." Since God is the only deity who is truly holy, He is the only one who formulates the terms for being in His category.

I love the old hymn, "When the Saints Go Marching In." The chorus says, "Lord, I want to be in that number, when the saints go marching in."[3] Someday our position as a saint will be actualized. We will no longer be in a body of sin and death, but we will have new bodies that can never sin again. What a wonderful day that will be. Let's go and march as saints.

---

[3]. Original author unknown.

Do You Have A Dagon?

"Now the Philistines took the ark of God and brought it from Ebenezer to Ashdod" (1 Samuel 5:1).

It had been a most gruesome battle between the Philistines and the Hebrews. Many had died and the Philistines were the victors. There was rejoicing in the camp of the uncircumcised Philistines and they took many spoils, including the symbol and strength of the Hebrews—the ark of God.

With great pageantry, the Philistines paraded the ark up the hill to their temple in Ashdod. They placed the ark beside the statue of Dagon, their heathen god. After all, the God of the Hebrews was just another god.

Early the next morning, the priests of Dagon entered the temple to worship. "What is this?" One of the priests gasped. "Look! Dagon has fallen in front of the ark of the Hebrew God."

"Quickly! Set him up before anyone sees," said another. "This was a trick of the gods."

The priests performed their religious duties without mentioning the incident of the fallen idol, but each time they walked in front of Dagon, they made sure to allow plenty of room. These priests had heard the story of Dagon and Samson who had been one of the Hebrew judges. Samson had been betrayed by Delilah into the hands of the Philistines. He had been taken to their prison and forced to work as a slave. When they brought Samson out to entertain them, his God had restored Samson's strength and he was able to pull the pillars from under the temple and the whole building, including Dagon, was dashed to pieces, killing everyone. That story was embedded in their minds.

The priests had a restless night and rose early the next morning. What met their eyes was horrifying. Dagon had not only fallen before the ark of the Hebrew God, but he was also decapitated and both hands were gone! The priests hurried from the temple to tell their lords. To make the situation worse, the men of Ashdod were ravaged with festering tumors. It was decided to remove the ark from the temple of Dagon to the city of Gath, but the men of Gath were smitten with the same tumors. The curse of the Hebrew God was more than they could stand. They knew the ark must be returned to Israel as quickly as possible.

***

You can read the rest of this interesting story to find out how the priests delivered the ark back to Israel. It's not wise to fall into the hands of the living God.

You can find many portions of Scripture where God declares that He is the only God of the universe and there is no other. The Hebrews were the only people who had a monotheistic religion. All the other nations had multiple gods they worshiped. In the Ten Commandments, God had told Moses that they were to have no other gods before Him. God warned them not to practice pluralism as the other nations did.

God also tells us that He is a jealous God. Does that sound strange to you? Read Deuteronomy 6:13-15: "You shall fear only the Lord your God; and you shall worship Him and swear by His name. You shall not follow other gods, any of the gods of the peoples who surround you, for the Lord your God in the midst of you is a jealous God; otherwise the anger of the Lord your God will be kindled against you, and He will wipe you off the face of the earth." Makes you glad we live in the age of grace. But since our God is the same yesterday, today, and tomorrow, He still feels the same way about those who have trusted in Him through Christ. No other god will stand beside Jehovah God.

What is your Dagon? What thing or things do you place beside God? That's different for each believer. We need to examine ourselves to make sure we're not serving some kind of Dagon. If we are, it won't stand. At some point, God will have to pluck it away and smash it to the ground. He is jealous for our whole being, and He should be. He gave His only Son to purchase us, and we belong to Him.

As Paul told the believers in Corinth, "Or do you not know that your body is a temple of the Holy Spirit who is in you, whom you have from God, and that you are not your own? For you have been bought with a price: therefore glorify God in your body" (1 Corinthians 6:19-20).

Jesus was asked by a lawyer what he needed to do to inherit eternal life. Jesus answered by asking the lawyer a question. Jesus asked him what the Law said. The lawyer responded, "'You shall love the Lord your God with all your heart, and with all your soul, and with all your strength, and with all your mind; and your neighbor as yourself.' And He [Jesus] said to him, 'You have answered correctly; do this and you will live'" (Luke 10:27-28).

Mary Baird

There is no room for other gods in the life of a believer. It might be a good idea to ask our heavenly Father to reveal any other gods we may be harboring so that we can discard them quickly.

Where Were You?

"Then the Lord answered Job out of the whirlwind and said, 'Who is this that darkens counsel by words without knowledge?'" (Job 38:1-2).

To me, an absolutely profound statement about God's sovereignty is found in the last chapters of the book of Job. And what makes them so marvelous is that they are spoken by God Himself.

Most believers are familiar with Job's story. He was a devout believer in God and made no secret about that fact. His whole life was devoted to living a life of holiness surrounded by a society of wickedness. Sounds familiar, doesn't it?

But Satan didn't like Job and wanted to destroy him. Satan came before God and put forth a challenge. He said that the only reason Job was faithful was because God had blessed him. After further discussion, God told Satan he could strike Job, but the one thing he could not do was kill him. Since Satan loves to destroy, this was music to his ears. Job became the battleground between Satan and God. You can read about the devastation Satan brought on Job and his family in chapters 1 and 2.

The next chapters tell about Job's good friends who were determined to blame Job for all his problems. They believed that if Job would simply come clean and confess his sins, God would restore him. If you've ever had a sibling blame you for something you didn't do and been chastised for it by your parents, you know exactly how Job felt.

To his credit, Job stood by his virtue and argued with his friends. We all admire Job's tenacity throughout all his losses. Even his wife told him to curse God and die. She'd lost all her children, all her possessions, and her elevated standing in the community. I have a feeling she wondered herself if Job had done some horrible thing and they were both being punished for it.

For a while Job is able to maintain his integrity and keep the proper perspective regarding the goodness of God. But as the days, hours, and minutes of agony continue—not to mention the constant ranting of his friends—Job begins to waver. He's ready to die because he doesn't understand why the God he worshiped and held in a lofty position would put him through such torment. In despair, Job cries out, "Oh that I had one to hear me! Behold, here is my signature; let the Almighty answer me! And the indictment which my adversary has written" (Job 31:35).

Ever feel that way? Have you ever gone through a trial that never seemed to end? You prayed and prayed, but God was silent. You began to doubt God, and like Job, you wondered why you were ever born.

The seminary lessons now begin and they are conducted by God Himself. "Then the Lord answered Job out of the whirlwind and said" (Job 38:1), Get ready, Job. Gird up your loins and hold on. I am going to ask you a series of questions, and the heading for all of them is "Where were you?" Read chapters 38, 39, 40 and 41 and you'll hear the questions. God ends with this statement, "Will the faultfinder contend with the Almighty? Let him who reproves God answer it" (Job 40:2).

Come, Let Us Reason Together

The fascinating part of this story is that God knew there was a problem area in Job's life that even he did not know existed. We're not told what that was, but Job knew and he answered God in chapter 42. The very end of his confession is this, "I have heard of You by the hearing of the ear; but now my eye sees You; therefore I retract, and I repent in dust and ashes" (Job 42:5-6). If you miss the ending to this story, you'll miss one of the best parts.

When I'm tempted to doubt God's magnificence and wisdom, I ask myself, "Where were you, Mary." It brings me back to reality every time.

Faith Whiteout

> "For in hope we have been saved, but hope that is seen is not hope; for who hopes for what he already sees? But if we hope for what we do not see, with perseverance we wait eagerly for it (Romans 8:24-25).

Our family recently took a skiing vacation in the superlative mountains of Colorado. As we left Denver and began our climb up the Rockies, it began to snow. The higher we went, the denser the snow became. Everyone in the van had fallen asleep except me, and my son who was driving. I enjoyed watching the mountains become snow-packed while the soft flakes fell against the back window where I was seated.

As we continued our climb, the falling snow hid the view from my eyes. I glanced at the front windows to see if my son could see the highway ahead. Although it was difficult, it seemed that he was doing a fine job keeping on track. I leaned my head back on the head rest and relaxed for a moment. From time to time I'd glance back at the front windows to see how things were looking.

As I made my usual momentary look at the front window, we became completely engulfed with blankets of snow, and out the front windows was solid white. I'd been in heavy rains and even fog, but this was different. It seemed as if some unseen hand had wrapped our van in a solid white sheet, and for a second, I was paralyzed. I let out a gasp which awakened my other son sitting in the passenger seat and he too let out a cry. This woke the others and all of us were scared beyond belief. Here we were high up in the mountains on a twisting turning highway and could see nothing. If we stopped, we took the chance of someone hitting us from behind, but to go forward was to chance hitting a rail and going over the side of the mountain. My son slowed the car to a crawl, but he had no idea which way to steer the van.

Just as quickly as the snow blinded us, it was gone. My son could see the highway again and was able to speed up and be on our way. We all breathed a prayer of thanksgiving to God for keeping us safe during those frantic seconds of total blindness. Later my sons told me we had been in a "whiteout," which is a common occurrence in the mountains during a blowing snow shower.

For some reason, that incident reminded me of Romans 8:24-25 and 2 Corinthians 5:7. The second verse says, "For we walk by faith, not by sight." Those verses took on a new meaning for me. I don't like being blindsided. I'm pragmatic, so I have a hard time when I can't see what's in front of me.

God says that we honor Him by having faith in Him when we cannot see. It shows us and others that we trust Him completely. He tells us that He will lead and guide us through "faith whiteouts" in our life. Those are the times when nothing makes sense to us, and we can't see the reason why.

We think that those things which we can see are reality, but we are told by Apostle Paul in 2 Corinthians 4:17-18, "For the momentary, light affliction is producing for us an eternal weight of glory far beyond all comparison, while we look not at the things which are seen, but at the things which are not seen; for the things which are seen are temporal, but the things which are not seen are eternal." Did you get the force of that statement? The Christian walk must be one of trust and faith. The world tells us that "seeing is believing," but God tells us that "believing is seeing."

The Portico of Solomon

"It was winter, and Jesus was walking in the temple in
the portico of Solomon" (John 10:23).

The cold air bit deeply into their skin even though their cloaks were pulled tightly around them. The covered porch with its tall pillars offered little protection from the cold Jerusalem winter, but as new men arrived for the Feast of Dedication and gathered around the rabbi, it became bearable.

The looks on the faces of the Jews gave Jesus an idea of what was coming. Another confrontation would surely ensue. There had been many such meetings on this porch over the past three years. Anytime the rabbi Jesus showed up, the other Jewish scholars wanted to debate the teachings of this upstart carpenter with a questionable background. It was said He was illegitimate, but His greatest offence was that He questioned Jewish laws. They were also jealous of His popularity with the people. It was true that there were reports of unusual miracles He had performed, but that could just as easily have been a satanic gift and not from Jehovah God. The latest rumor was that Jesus was professing to be the promised Savior of Israel—the Messiah!

"How long will you keep us in suspense? If you are the Christ, tell us plainly." With anger in their voices, they began to press Him for an answer. It was time for a showdown to once and for all display this man as a fraud.

***

Mary Baird

During the days Jesus was on earth, the portico of Solomon was one of the few remaining parts of the great temple Solomon had built while king of Israel. It was a popular meeting place and the Messiah walked and taught there many times. On this particular day, the claims of Jesus would be elevated to a new high and they would try to stone him to death for His words. It was the beginning of the end.

After the death, resurrection, and ascension of Jesus, Peter became the leader of the small band of believers. In Acts 3:11 Peter's second great sermon is preached from the portico of Solomon. Peter is arrested for teaching that Jesus was indeed the promised Messiah and that He was resurrected from the dead. Peter went on to tell the Jews that they had killed their own Savior, and if they did not repent and acknowledge who Christ was, they would be utterly destroyed. Again in Acts 5:12 it is recorded that the Apostles did many signs and wonders in Solomon's portico. They were all arrested, given a flogging, and warned to stop preaching such nonsense.

We all must make our way back to the portico of Solomon and determine which way we will go. On that cold winter day as Jesus talked and made claims to be divine, do we pick up stones to kill him? As Peter and the other apostles preached the Christ, His resurrection, and salvation through no one else, do we flog the messenger and refuse to believe? Jesus is or is not what He and His followers claimed. As you stand on that porch and hear the testimony, you too must make that decision.

Our Three Inch Rudder

"And the tongue is a fire, the very world of iniquity; the tongue is set among our members as that which defiles the entire body, and sets on fire the course of our life, and is set on fire by hell" (James 3:6).

If I were to ask you to name the sins in your life that caused you a lot of trouble, I bet you could think of them quickly. We've all had to live with the hurtful outcome of certain transgressions. But there is one source of sin that we seldom give a lot of thought—the sin of the tongue.

I've never done much boating, but I do know that even the largest ships have a rudder hidden beneath the water whereby the navigator steers the ship in the direction he wishes to go.

James, the half-brother of Jesus, spends a lot of time on the power of the tongue. In James 3:1-12, he gives us some strong teaching on the words that come out of our mouth. He compares the tongue to the rudder on a big ship. "Look at the ships also, though they are so great and are driven by strong winds, are still directed by a very small rudder, wherever the inclination of the pilot desires. So also the tongue is a small part of the body, and yet it boasts of great things" (James 3:4-5a). But the statement I wish to focus on is found in James 3:6, "And the tongue is a fire, the very world of iniquity; the tongue is set among our members as that which defiles the entire body, and sets on fire the course of our life, and is set on fire by hell." If I understand this statement correctly, the tongue can actually guide our lives in the direction of total waste and misery.

I have known marriages torn apart by the tongue of either the husband or wife through complaining, criticizing, demeaning comments, lying, and the demand for hypothetical rights. Divorce was certainly not the course of life wished by either party when the marriage began, but because of the tongue, that course was ultimately achieved. Or take the child who hears only pessimistic and judgmental words from his parents while growing up, then becomes rebellious and begins using drugs or chooses other unhealthy activities. The parents didn't want these problems and hurts for their child, but the tongue helped guide them there anyway.

Have you ever seen a church split apart by wagging tongues? The venom of false accusations or outright lies has sent many a once dynamic church into oblivion as far as its usefulness is concerned. "A gentle answer turns away wrath, but a harsh word stirs up anger" (Proverbs 15:1). Or have you seen reputations hauled through the mud by gossip? The worst is gossip passed around disguised as prayer. That's when we gather together, and bring up people we pretend to be concerned about for prayer. We air all their problems and sin before the group, and then hopefully have time left to pray. Wisely did the man say, "Death and life are in the power of the tongue, and those who love it will eat its fruit" (Proverbs 18:21).

Both Paul and Peter warn the Christian community to "attend to their own business" (1 Thessalonians 4:11), and to not be "troublesome meddlers" (1 Peter 4:15). I couldn't help but notice that Peter lumps troublesome meddlers in with murderers, thieves and evildoers.

Come, Let Us Reason Together

If you've ever been the object of lies, you'll understand better the psalmist who says, "Deliver my soul, O Lord, from lying lips, from a deceitful tongue" (Psalms 120:2).

James closes his teaching on the tongue by saying, "But no one can tame the tongue; it is a restless evil and full of deadly poison. With it we bless our Lord and Father; and with it we curse men, who have been made in the likeness of God; from the same mouth come both blessing and cursing. My brethren, these things ought not to be this way" (James 3:8-10). Indeed, they should not.

The tongue is a very small part of our body, and yet it can guide us into places we'd rather not go. Words spoken in haste, anger, jealousy, or unkindness can set off a chain reaction we soon regret. And the trouble with words is that you cannot take them back once they leave your mouth. We all need to pray, "Let the words of my mouth and the meditation of my heart be acceptable in Your sight, O Lord, my rock and my Redeemer" (Psalms 19:14).

By the Hair of Your Chinny Chin Chin

"For no man can lay a foundation other than the one which is laid, which is Jesus Christ. Now if any man builds upon the foundation with gold, silver, precious stones, wood, hay, straw, each man's work will become evident; for the day will show it because it is to be revealed with fire, and the fire itself will test the quality of each man's work" (1 Corinthians 3:11-13).

The Apostle Paul explained to the church in Corinth how rewards were given by God in heaven. We don't always think about that aspect of our Christian lives, but we should. As believers, the life and work we do here on earth will be important when we stand before our Lord.

There are two types of works—those that can withstand the fire of testing and those that will not. You can accumulate gold, silver, and precious stones. Those types of works can withstand heat. Paul does not name what works these might be, but we can be sure they glorified the Lord and benefited other people. They would have been performed with the proper attitude and without self-interest. Perhaps the works were never noticed by anyone or even appreciated as they should have been. Perhaps they were sacrificial and caused great pain to the giver. Maybe they were relationships that we worked hard to preserve even when our instincts told us to give up. Some will be those who left comfort and family to serve on a foreign missionary field, and even lost their lives for doing so. The rewarded gifts will be based on quality, not quantity.

The next set of works is wood, hay, and straw. We all know what happens to that material when it meets with fire. It goes up in a puff of smoke and nothing is left but black ashes. Those types of works will not withstand the heat of scrutiny. I have a feeling those works may have had the approval and recognition of others here on earth, but not before God. Jesus told his disciples that the religious leaders of his day arrogantly paraded around with their prayer cards and little bells on the bottom of their robes; they put ashes on their faces so the people would know they were fasting; and they made a big show of giving a tenth of everything. Jesus said they had already received their reward.

Anyone who has truly received Christ as Savior will be in heaven, but they may have nothing worthy of reward. They'll stand and watch as others receive recognition for humble service.

I have a theory in regard to rewards that may or may not be true. In Revelation 4:10-11, we are told that the twenty-four elders fall down before the throne of our Lord and then they do an interesting thing. They cast their crowns before the throne, saying "Worthy are You, our Lord and our God, to receive glory and honor and power" (Revelation 4:11a). I wonder if the rewards we receive in heaven will be given back to the Lord in honor of Him who died for us. Perhaps it will be similar to the wise men who brought gifts at His birth. If all our works are burned, we will stand empty handed on that momentous day.

Mary Baird

So the questions is—do we want to get into heaven by the hair of our chinny chin chin, or do we want to receive further recognition and have a gift to offer our Lord? I pray that I won't be left out of that privilege.

Divine Humor

"He who sits in the heavens laughs, the Lord scoffs at them" (Psalms 2:4).

Have you ever wondered what makes God laugh? I realize that God is spirit, but He often uses human terms to describe Himself. As finite beings, we could never comprehend God in His real essence. So, God condescends to describe Himself in concepts we can understand.

Through the years, I've seen or heard about those who flaunt their anti-God rhetoric and even dare God to do something about it. I heard of a man who blatantly denied there was a God, shook his fist toward heaven, and declared that if there was a God He should strike him dead. When nothing happened, the man bragged that he had proven God did not exist.

In Psalms 2:1-12 we have a panoramic history of mankind's determination and the length they'll go to rid themselves of any god. If there is a god, they reason, and especially the God of Scripture, then man must be subservient to Him. He must come to terms with his sin and rebellion and realize that his existence depends on pleasing his master. That is unthinkable to the arrogant human race. The terminology of this psalm is astonishing. Notice that the people are in an uproar. They are so angry that they'll do anything to liberate themselves from the supposed chains of God.

Mary Baird

From the time Adam and Eve left the garden in disgrace, the battle has been fierce. Down through the pages of Scripture, we see man defying God at every turn. But the final battle took place on a rocky hill in Jerusalem some two thousand years ago. A man hung between heaven and hell. Our arch enemy, Satan, was about to meet his final destruction, but he didn't give up easily.

In our psalm, we are told the conclusion of that battle. Isn't that amazing? Hundreds of years before the event even happened, we are told how it ends. Mankind stands with their fists raised toward heaven against the Lord and His Anointed (Jesus) and swears their refusal to worship. Do you know what God does? He laughs and scoffs at their puniness. The word *scoff* is interesting. It means "to show, or treat with, insolent ridicule or mockery."[4] To God, this is humorous. It reminds me of a tiny grass snake no bigger than a giant worm I saw in our front yard. When I leaned down to take a closer look, it reared up its head and opened its small mouth in defiance. I couldn't help but laugh thinking how easily I could destroy that snake.

Did you know that God also finds it humorous when evil men plot against His people? Those who belong to God are precious in His sight and when the wicked try to destroy us, God laughs at them. In Psalms 37:12-13 it says, "The wicked plots against the righteous and gnashes at him with his teeth. The Lord laughs at him, for He sees his day is coming." Don't misunderstand. God takes our pain and grief from evil men seriously. The point of this psalm is to remind us that we may suffer here on earth, but we will be vindicated in eternity, and those who sought our destruction will themselves be destroyed.

---

4. *Webster's Collegiate Dictionary*, s.v., "scoff."

Come, Let Us Reason Together

I'm amused at the thought of God laughing at brazen men when they rebel and refuse to acknowledge Him who sits on the throne of the universe. How arrogant and foolish. Can't you just see man in an absolute uproar against God? Just like that grass snake, one word from God and they'd be gone. I have to admit—I find that humorous myself.

Do You Know I AM?

"And God said to Moses, 'I AM WHO I AM'; and He said, 'Thus shall you say to the sons of Israel, "I AM has sent me to you."'" (Exodus 3:14).

Moses is one of the greatest people in the Bible. Everyone who knows anything about Scripture knows who Moses is. He's the one who held up his staff and parted the Red Sea by the power of God so that the Hebrews could cross over and be saved from Pharaoh's army. But let's go further back than that to a time in the life of Moses when he was very happy tending sheep and raising his family in the land of Midian. His days of fighting were over after being forced to flee Egypt for killing an Egyptian. His privileged life as a prince in Egypt had came to a sudden end, and now he was a simple shepherd.

God turned Moses upside down by selecting him to return to Egypt. He was to free the Hebrews from slavery. Moses offered every kind of excuse for not going, but God would not take no for an answer. In desperation Moses offered his first excuse. He didn't know what God's name was and therefore would have no credibility before the people. God said His name was I AM. That sounds strange to us, but it fits God perfectly.

God is the I AM of everything.

When the Lord Jesus Christ came to earth as a man, He filled in some of the blanks regarding what I AM means. Jesus said I am the way, the truth, and the life (John 14:6); I am the bread of life (John 6:35); I am the good shepherd (John 10:11); I am the resurrection and the life (John 11:25); I am the vine and you are the branches (John 15:5); I am the light of the world (John 8:12); before Abraham was, I am (John 8:58); and I am the door of the sheep (John 10:7). And perhaps the most amazing I AM is found in John 18:4-6. It was the night of our Lord's betrayal and He was in the garden when Judas and the soldiers came to arrest Him. Jesus asked them "Whom do you seek?" and they answered "Jesus the Nazarene." Jesus answered them, "I am He (literally I AM)." That's not a threatening answer or an obstinate reply, but there was so much power in those words that the soldiers fell to the ground in total dismay. Can you imagine what would have happened if Jesus had decided not to go with them? One word of rebuke from our Lord and they would have disintegrated into ashes.

We, as believers, worship no ordinary God. There are other gods in the religious world, but they are false and meaningless. Only the God of Scripture is the I AM.

Over and over in the Old Testament, God proclaims Himself as the only true and all-powerful God. One such claim is in Isaiah 46:9-10, "Remember the former things long past, for I am God and there is no other; I am God and there is no one like Me, declaring the end from the beginning and from ancient times things which have not been done, saying, 'My purpose will be established, and I will accomplish all My good pleasure.'"

Do you know the I AM? If not, I challenge you to study Scripture and see for yourself. Put Him to the test and find out what a marvelous God we have.

Easter's Guarantee

"If God is for us, who is against us?" (Romans 8:31b).

One of my favorite Easter passages is found in Romans 8:31-37. It's not the one we usually think of as pertaining to the death and resurrection of Jesus, but it outlines some important facts regarding the sacrificial work of our Lord.

The section begins by asking a series of questions. In order to understand why the writer of Romans asks these questions, you'll need to go back and read what precedes it. An argument is given regarding our victory as a believer in a world of hatred toward God's children, and the fact that even when suffering, God is there to work everything out for our good and His glory.

After making his argument that God loves us, the writer of Romans reiterates the depth of that love by reminding us that God did not spare His own Son to give us our freedom from sin. God delivered Jesus as a sacrifice to a horrible humiliating death on a Roman cross. You cannot argue with that kind of love, and if you can accept that, then ask yourself, "If God was willing to give His Son for me, then why would He withhold anything good from me?" We may have problems here on earth, but we are to keep our focus on the promises given us for eternity.

The answer to the first question, "If God is for us, who is against us," is answered by another question, "Who will bring a charge against God's elect?" We can answer with a resounding, "Nobody!" Neither Satan, our worldly enemies, or even ourselves can bring a charge against us. "God is the one who justified. Who is the one who condemns?"

We are told in verse thirty-four that Jesus is the one who paid the ultimate price for us, sits by the right hand of God, and now intercedes for us. Do we really think that God would dishonor His Son by rejecting us at some point?

But let's be clear. This section is for believers in Jesus Christ. It's not for those who have rejected Him, or for those who are indifferent toward Him. In the same way as God would not dishonor His Son by rejecting those who trust in Him, God will not allow anyone to bypass His Son in receiving forgiveness. God does not accept Universalism—the belief that ultimately everyone will be saved whether they receive Christ or not.[5] The only way God will or can justify us is when we receive the gift of His Son's sacrifice in our place. And that justification is a guarantee.

---

5. *Webster's Collegiate Dictionary*, s.v., "Universalism."

Is Prosperity a Handicap?

"Woman received back their dead by resurrection; and others were tortured, not accepting their release, so that they might obtain a better resurrection; and others experienced mockings and scourgings, yes, also chains and imprisonment. They were stoned, they were sawn in two, they were tempted, they were put to death with the sword; they went about in sheepskins, in goatskins, being destitute, afflicted, ill-treated (men of whom the world was not worthy), wandering in deserts and mountains and caves and holes in the ground" (Hebrews 11:35-38).

I don't know about you, but these verses from the book of Hebrews make me shudder. It would be just fine with me to stick with the previous verses of this passage. Tell me about conquering kingdoms, obtaining promises, and putting armies to flight. Tell me what glories await me in eternity. Tell me how God is my protector and provider, but don't tell me to, "Consider it all joy, my brethren, when you encounter various trials," as James tells us. The only problem is that I can't find anywhere in Scripture where it says, "Consider it all joy, my brethren, when you encounter various and great prosperity."

The sin nature never changes; it never improves or learns its lesson. It never sits down and analyzes, or looks back over time and experiences to come to rational conclusions. Given the same set of circumstances and the same emotional conditions, it will tend toward repeating the same sin over and over.

Come, Let Us Reason Together

How often have we heard (or how often have we said), "It's easy to trust God in the good times, but very difficult to trust Him in the bad times"? I've been thinking about that lately, and my consensus has changed just a little. You must admit that when trials come our way, God does become prominent in our minds, even if we're questioning Him or feeling angry with Him. At the very least, we're looking upward and not outward. Where apathy and superficial and hollow religious activity may have existed, we now focus on God. When our lives appear to be secure and safe, we can easily become confident in earthly things to sustain us.

Someone said that the highest form of insult is indifference. Our Lord said in Revelation 3:15-16, "I know your deeds; that you are neither cold nor hot; I wish that you were cold or hot. So because you are lukewarm, and neither hot nor cold, I will spit you out of My mouth." And this was a very rich group of believers to whom He was speaking! They were arrogantly saying, "I am rich, and have become wealthy; I have need of nothing."

Our Creator God knows us so well, doesn't He? In Deuteronomy 8:1-18, God, through his spokesperson Moses, warns the children of Israel as they prepare to enter the land of promise to not forget who brought them across miles of desert and defeated their enemies. Moses tells them that when they are sitting in a nice house they didn't build, and eating food they didn't farm, watching their flocks and their silver and their gold multiply, not to forget just who made all that happen by saying to themselves, "My power and the strength of my hand made me this wealth" (Deuteronomy 8:17b). I think we all know from reading further that they did forget.

Mary Baird

We often credit Satan for more intelligence than he deserves. In the book of Job, Satan appears before God with a challenge. He told God that Job was faithful to God because of all the prosperity God had given to him. He told God that if everything was taken away, Job would curse God. So, God allowed Satan to take everything from Job and leave him in an ash heap with sores over his entire body.

At first, Job shows forth his faith in God and we appropriately admire him for that. However, as Job's three friends continue to accuse him wrongly, and the agony of his condition seems to have no end, one little flaw begins to appear from Job's character that only God knew about, and only this trial could have revealed. Job admits that some of his faithfulness toward God stemmed from an external motive. He says in Job 42:5-6, "I have heard of You by the hearing of the ear; but now my eye sees You; therefore I retract, and I repent in dust and ashes." What Satan thought would be the ruination of Job turned out to bring Job a deeper, more meaningful relationship with the One he said he trusted.

Twenty or so years ago, my birth state of Oklahoma was at the height of oil producing opulence—perhaps one of the biggest in the history of this oil rich, red dirt country. People lived high and haughty. Then, just as quickly, it was over. Oil well servicing companies went out of business like rats off a sinking ship. Bankruptcies, foreclosures, and business closings became the norm. I was amused one day when I saw a bumper sticker on the back of a truck that read, "Dear God, if you'll give us one more chance, we'll do better." Do you think they would?

Paul the Apostle makes a statement in Philippians 4:11-12. He tells his readers that he had learned to be content in whatever circumstance he found himself. That's interesting enough, but in verse 12 he says "I have learned the secret of being filled and going hungry, both of having abundance and suffering need." The secret? What secret? And notice that he learned the secret. Who wouldn't want contentment in any situation of life, and who wouldn't want the secret of how to find that? What a study that would be.

An astute man once wrote, "Two things I asked of You [God], do not refuse me before I die: Keep deception and lies far from me, give me neither poverty nor riches; feed me with the food that is my portion, that I not be full and deny You and say, 'Who is the Lord?' Or that I not be in want and steal, and profane the name of my God" (Proverbs 30:7-9).

Is anything wrong with prosperity? Of course not! God is the one who blesses us with everything we have. But there is a warning attached to being wealthy because you'll have a harder time walking by faith. It will be a handicap. "Instruct those who are rich in this present world not to be conceited or to fix their hope on the uncertainty of riches, but on God, who richly supplies us with all things to enjoy" (1 Timothy 6:17).

Of Cattle and Kings

"Now I, Nebuchadnezzar, praise, exalt and honor the King of heaven, for all His works are true and His ways just, and He is able to humble those who walk in pride" (Daniel 4:37).

The king walked slowly around the roof of his palace overlooking the magnificence of his empire. His main palace was located near the Euphrates River and had cedar beams for the roof and glazed tile for the walls. He had adorned the building with gold, silver, and precious stones. He could see his other two palaces in the distance—one which was used as a museum to house all his trophies. He thought about the processional way that was seventy feet wide between beautiful walls of glazed tiles covered with paintings of lions. The king had constructed the passageway; it was used for the New Year festival honoring Murduk, one of the Babylonian gods.

"All this I have done by my power and for my majesty," the King said as he continued inventory of his vast empire. "Who else is as powerful and wise as me?"

As the words left his mouth, a thundering voice came from heaven and said, "King Nebuchadnezzar, to you it is declared: sovereignty has been removed from you, and you will be driven away from mankind, and your dwelling place will be with the beasts of the field" (Daniel 4:31b-32a).

Come, Let Us Reason Together

For the next seven years this once powerful and boastful ruler of the known world was forced into the wilderness to eat grass like cattle and grow hair and nails like an eagle. In one swift stroke of God's finger, Nebuchadnezzar was reduced to rubble.

The ending of this story is the best, and it's exciting to read what happened to this king at the close of those seven years.

Looking around us, we see there is no shortage of arrogant people, and unfortunately some of them are in leadership positions. They cause untold misery to those over whom they wield power, thinking themselves smarter and worthier to live above the common people. They have little or no regard for anyone; they consider themselves invincible.

Throughout history, God has given us a picture of how impotent man is, and the account of Nebuchadnezzar is one of the best. Every breath we take is given us by God and we have no power whatsoever unless God commands it.

There is another such story, although not as dramatic, given in Acts 12:20-23. Another king claimed to be a divine being. God didn't give him the opportunity to repent; God just struck him dead.

When you stop and think about it, man has not changed from the very beginning. After being told they could be like God, Adam and Eve willingly picked fruit from the tree of good and evil forbidden them by their Creator. Wanting to possess power through position is as old as the book of Genesis.

Man's value system says grab everything you can, claw your way to the top, look out for number one, use people for your own advancement; God's value system says, "Therefore humble yourself under the mighty hand of God, that He may exalt you at the proper time" (1 Peter 5:6).

Lie from Hell

"Now while they were on their way, some of the guard came into the city and reported to the chief priests all that had happened. And when they had assembled with the elders and counseled together, they gave a large sum of money to the soldiers, and said, 'You are to say "His disciples came by night and stole Him away while we were asleep." And if this should come to the governor's ears, we will win him over and keep you out of trouble.' And they took the money and did as they had been instructed; and this story was widely spread among the Jews, and is to this day" (Matthew 28:11-15).

Have you ever known anyone who would rather believe a lie than the truth even if the truth were staring them right in the face? It's one thing to be deceived and tell a lie but another to lie when you know differently.

The greatest lie ever told is found in our passage in Matthew. For months Jesus had been telling people He was going to be killed, but He would rise on the third day. No one believed Him, including His disciples. Jesus was crucified and verifiably pronounced dead according to a Roman centurion who knew his business. The religious leaders were afraid that somehow the disciples of Jesus would steal His body and declare Jesus had risen from the dead. They commissioned Pilate to help them prevent this and guards were stationed at the entrance of the boulder covering the opening of Jesus' tomb. Additionally, a seal was placed on it and everyone knew that breaking the seal of Rome would mean death.

It's really funny to think the religious leaders would be so concerned about the disciples stealing Jesus' body. The disciples were terrified after seeing what happened to their leader; all their hopes had been dashed. Only the women went to the grave site that morning. The men were still hiding, fearing they might be the next ones arrested and crucified. Why on earth would you risk your life to perpetrate a lie knowing it was a lie and possibly die in the process?

I would love to have been at the grave of Jesus the morning of His resurrection. We don't know how many guards were standing watch, but there were several. I have a feeling they were anxious for the third day to come so they could get off work.

Sometime before daylight, the earth gave a stressful heave; an angel of God descended like lightning and rolled the stone away as if it were a rubber ball. Then, just to show how simple it was, the angel sat on the stone as if to say, "Well, that was easy." No wonder the guards were frozen with fear.

I have a feeling that after it was all over, and everyone had left the area, the guards had a discussion. Some of them needed to go and report to the Jewish religious leaders and tell them what had happened. They didn't want to report to Pilate just yet because they would be in a lot of trouble for allowing the body to disappear. These guards told the priests exactly what took place that morning—the earthquake, the angel, the rolled boulder, and the empty tomb. I imagine they left out no detail even down to how frightened they were. They had to make these religious leaders believe them in order to maintain their integrity as guards.

After hearing what happened, the religious leaders made a monumental decision. They decided to pay off the guards; they concocted a false story, and had the soldiers circulate that lie. It's almost breathtaking to think about. At least they should have been a little curious about this man who claimed to be from God, who had performed countless miracles, and who had taught as no man had ever taught. Even the Roman rulers could find nothing worthy of death for this man. You'd think that the Jewish priests might want to investigate and find out if he really came back to life. But then, that's the deceitfulness of Satan.

We have the same situation today. Christianity has survived untold attempts to put a stop to its truth. Jesus Christ shows Himself in so many ways, but Satan blinds people so they do not see the truth.

Today they've become more sophisticated with that original story. When asked how Jesus was seen alive after his death by over 500 people, the disbelievers have come up with the "swoon theory." They say the disciples stole the body alright, but Jesus was never really dead. When put in the tomb, the dampness of the cave revived Him, and He was seen walking around. Seriously? Jesus was beaten beyond recognition with a nail spiked whip that tore His flesh from his bones; His beard was pulled out by the roots, a crown of long stemmed thorns was pushed deep into His head; He was nailed by His hands and feet to a wooden cross for hours, and His side pierced with a Roman sword as both blood and water came out. There is no telling how much blood He lost beforehand during all that torture. It would take more faith for me to believe Jesus survived all that than the proven truth of His resurrection.

If, in fact, Jesus did rise from the dead, how should that impact our lives? Should we shrug our shoulders and walk away? Or would the better part of common sense tell us we need to investigate this further. The book of John is a great place to start if you're seeking to know the truth. May God open the eyes of those who are still blinded by the greatest lie ever told.

Proof Beyond Belief

"And behold, the veil of the temple was torn in two from top to bottom...The tombs were opened; and many bodies of the saints...were raised...Now the centurion, and those who were with him...when they saw the earthquake and the things that were happening, became very frightened and said, 'Truly this was the Son of God'" (Matthew 27:51-54).

We don't often think about what happened the moment our Lord gave up His Spirit in death, but it must have been devastating for those looking on. We learn from Luke that at the moment Christ was dying, one of the criminals being crucified next to Christ recognized Jesus was Messiah and said, "Remember me when You come in Your kingdom" (Luke 23:42).

In our Matthew passage, the hardened Roman soldiers acknowledged that Jesus was the Son of God. The tall, thick, tapestry curtain in the Jewish temple separating men from God was torn in two—top to bottom—signifying that man now had access to Jehovah God. And the crowd began beating their breasts as they walked away. Tombs were opened and dead people walked out of their burial prisons. Something universal had happened on that hill at Golgotha, and many realized they had taken part in a divine battle of unprecedented proportions. This was no ordinary man, and this was no ordinary death.

Come, Let Us Reason Together

But something even more amazing was going to happen on the first day of the Jewish week. The man, Jesus, who had been crucified, was resurrected by God, and several hundred people saw Him alive. Jesus ate, fellowshipped, and taught His disciples forty days before returning to His heavenly Father (Acts 1:1-3). He also gave them an incredible promise—He would come again.

Many years have come and gone since that day, and mockers still ask "Where is the promise of His coming?" If miraculous happenings accompanied His death, what do you think will accompany His return? We get a glimpse of that magnificent day in Revelation 19:11-16. He won't come as the sacrificial lamb again, but as a conquering king. Are you prepared for His return?

Spiritual Babies

> "And I, brethren, could not speak to you as to spiritual men, but as to men of flesh, as to infants in Christ. I gave you milk to drink, not solid food; for you were not yet able to receive it. Indeed, even now you are not yet able, for you are still fleshly. For since there is jealousy and strife among you, are you not fleshly, and are you not walking like mere men?" (1 Corinthians 3:1-3).

We have several new babies in our church body. I love to watch them as they grow from tiny infants to toddlers slowly making their way down the hallways trying to stay balanced on their wobbly feet. During the service, they laugh or cry out loud or make cooing noises until their mothers must take them out. They have no social skills and could care less about anyone but themselves. Their diet consists of bland pureed food that looks horrible to us and gets into every crevice of their faces so that a good washing is needed after each meal.

Everyone loves babies even when they're messy. But if a normal child the age of ten still behaves like an infant, it certainly isn't cute. It turns us off completely. The Apostle Paul writes a letter to the church at Corinth and instructs them to grow up. They had been taught by Paul, who was perhaps the greatest teacher of doctrine who ever lived except for the Lord, but the believers at Corinth were acting like infants. Rather than becoming spiritual adults, these believers were whining and crying, still eating pabulum, fighting each other as children would over a toy, and causing division in the church.

Food for the baby Christian is called milk and food for the more mature is called meat. Paul doesn't say what those two spiritual food items represent, but most think that milk is the simple plan of salvation while meat represents a deeper understanding of God's Word. It's the stuff that takes hard study and a relentless searching of the pages of Scripture to wrestle with issues that force us to think.

Just as a new born baby needs the nourishment of the mother's milk in order to grow, so too a new born believer needs the milk of the Word to grow. In fact, the Apostle Peter says in his letter, "Like newborn babes, long for the pure milk of the word, that by it you may grow in respect to salvation" (1 Peter 2:2). However, Paul was displeased with the believers in the church at Corinth. They should have been able to handle meat, but had to stay on milk.

What are some signs of an immature believer? I think Paul was saying one sure indicator was how we treat other believers. If we are run by jealousy, elitism, strife, selfishness, and leadership identification, we know we've not matured.

A mature believer will not be led away by every new, ear-tingling doctrine that comes their way. Paul writes to the church in Ephesians 4:14-15, "As a result, we are no longer to be children, tossed here and there by waves and carried about by every wind of doctrine, by the trickery of men, by craftiness in deceitful scheming; but speaking the truth in love, we are to grow up in all aspects into Him who is the head, even Christ."

Mary Baird

God desires us to grow in our Christian walk. We need to put away our childish toys and mature so that we can serve others in humble obedience.

The Reluctant Saint

"And he fell to the ground and heard a voice saying to him, 'Saul, Saul, why are you persecuting Me?'" (Acts 9:4).

The distinguished looking man traversed the rocky roads on his five day trip to Damascus. The sun beat down on the band of men traveling together, but their mission was set in their hearts like a flint. No matter the difficulty or dangers on the road, the leader of this determined group of men would press on and nothing and no one would interfere with his assignment.

The leader lifted his hand and felt against his breast to make sure the letters for arrest given him by the high priest were still in place under his tunic. "I'll get these deserting troublemakers. They think they can avoid punishment for their blasphemy," He mumbled under his breath. *If necessary, I'll chase them to the ends of the earth. This new movement must be crushed as quickly as possible. We thought we had it stopped in Jerusalem by stoning Stephen, but since that proved ineffective, we must put greater pressure and a more severe punishment on them. From now on, no one—young or old—will be exempt. I'll make an example of those in Damascus and others will soon drop away.* The man's facial features became twisted and obdurate as he thought about the rebels who followed a false prophet named Jesus, and their insistence that He was the promised Messiah.

"What foolishness," the man snarled out the words. "Messiah, indeed! Why—he's dead—hung on a cross in the most humiliating manner known. What kind of Messiah would allow such a thing? The true Messiah will bring death to the Romans and restore Israel to her proper greatness. That man—that common carpenter was certainly not the Messiah we are looking for."

"Did you say something, Rabbi Saul?" One of the group of men headed for Damascus looked over at the leader of the posse. "Did you say something to me?"

Saul's mind jolted back and he realized his mumbling had become audible. "No…no, I was just thinking to myself. I'm anxious to get this over with and head back to Jerusalem with our prisoners."

"Sir, are you hungry?" Saul's servant asked. "It's midday, and we still have a little way to go before we reach Damascus. The heat of the day may have made you weak."

Saul was forming his answer when a radiance—a light that shown down with such brightness that the sun disappeared, surrounded him. Saul was engulfed by an illumination of radiance that was mystical. His legs became as feeble as reeds in the marshes and he fell to the ground in a lifeless heap, unable to move. Saul's intellectual mind tried to reason, but for once in his life, his mind was useless to him. All the study, philosophical thinking, and instruction he'd learned melted away by the awesome power of the moment. This was one time that Saul was not in control and had no answers.

In what seemed like an eternity to Saul, a voice of unprecedented majesty and authority finally spoke. The voice was as the sound of rushing water and as beautiful as a glorious choir. The words were simple, but penetratingly forceful. "Saul, Saul, why are you persecuting me?"

Saul looked into the light and saw a figure of a man clothed in radiant snow white linen. His expression was loving and kind, but it was his eyes that captured Saul. It was as if they penetrated his very soul and knew everything about him. Saul's words finally formed. "Who are you, Lord?" he managed to ask.

"I am Jesus whom you are persecuting, but get up and enter the city, and it will be told you what you must do."

Just as quickly as the light appeared, it was gone. Saul still lay on the ground for a moment and then rose to his feet. The other men rushed to his side, shaken by what had happened. They had seen the light and heard the voice, but could not make out the words and neither had they seen anyone. Saul blinked trying to focus, but realized he was blind. The others took his hand and guided him as they continued their journey. The rest of the trip to Damascus was one of silent bewilderment. No one wanted to talk about what had just happened because no one was sure—except for Saul.

***

If you read the rest of the supernatural conversion of Saul you would find that he does regain his sight and goes on to become the greatest evangelist the world has ever known. His name is changed to Paul, and he has left us with many letters filled with doctrine, encouragement, warnings, and instruction. There is no way this man would have come to Christ except for the divine intervention of God.

I must ask a question in regard to that. Would we have come to Christ except for the divine intervention of God? Our conversion may not have been as dramatic as Paul's, and may not be something worthy of writing down in a book, but we too were in rebellion against God. You may say that since Paul, after all, had actually killed believers, it took a greater miracle for him. But if you recall, Jesus tells us in the Gospels that if we hate our brother, we've committed murder too. Sin resides in our hearts, and our actions are only an expression of that. By the time our actions take place, sin has already been launched.

We are all reluctant saints. As our Lord said, "No one can come to Me unless the Father who sent Me draws him; and I will raise him up on the last day" (John 6:44). This truth should give us a renewed appreciation for our deliverance. None of us deserved the sacrifice Christ made for us, but He did it anyway. What a wonderful God and what a wonderful salvation.

Love's Anguish

"Surely our griefs He Himself bore, and our sorrows He carried" (Isaiah 53:4a).

If you've ever had a loved one in intensive care, you know what it's like to anguish through the night. When my father was dying, my sister and I spent the night in the ICU waiting room, but never slept. We sat anxiously waiting for the next visit to his room. He was unconscious and could not respond to us, but we held his hand and talked to him.

No matter how difficult our burden, we cannot imagine the agony our Lord faced the night of His arrest. We see Him in the garden of Gethsemane, and as we piece together the Gospels, we discover a small portion of the anguish our Lord endured. Listen—can you hear Him say, "My soul is deeply grieved?" Can you see the drops of blood on His forehead? Can you hear Him say to his disciples, "Could you not keep watch with Me one hour?" Can you hear Him ask His father, "My Father, if it is possible, let this cup pass from Me," and can you hear Him say, "Your will be done"?

We often think our Lord was agonizing about facing the physical pain, but it was far deeper than that. He was going to carry the sin of the world on Himself. In just a few hours, the Father would turn His back on His Son. At that moment, Christ experienced separation from God the Father for the first time ever because all the sin that ever existed was heaped on His shoulders. He was the innocent Holy One who died, not for Himself, but to free us. No wonder Jesus cried, "My God, My God, why have you forsaken Me?"

If we were to leave the story here, His death would have been pointless. But we know the rest of the story. Our Lord conquered death and He lives! Without the resurrection, Christ would have been just a good man dying at the hands of evil people. We are told in 1 Corinthians 15:13-14, "But if there is no resurrection of the dead, not even Christ has been raised; and if Christ has not been raised, then our preaching is vain, your faith also is vain." Then just a few verses later in verse 17 it says, "and if Christ has not been raised, your faith is worthless; you are still in your sins."

Jesus was willing to face the anguish of that terrible night because of His love for mankind. If we scorn and reject that anguish, we have only ourselves to blame for God's wrath. Christ willingly endured rejection, ridicule, cruelty, and a humiliating death, but not again. This is the moment, this is the time, and tomorrow may be too late. Believe and receive His forgiveness before you take another breath. The words are simple and direct.

Lord, I know I deserved to be on that cross because I'm a sinner. I accept you as my substitute. Thank you for loving me.

Which Way?

> "There is a way which seems right to a man, but its end is the way of death" (Proverbs 14:12).

Not long ago a friend of mine and I were driving to a shopping center. My friend took her car because she'd been there before and knew the way. As we drove along talking and laughing, it appeared to me that we should have been at our destination. I mentioned to her my concern and she pulled to the side of the road. After looking in all directions, she laughed and sheepishly admitted that she'd been going in the opposite direction of the shopping center. I knew she was embarrassed and I tried to assure her it happened to everyone. We made a hasty U-turn and finally arrived at the correct location.

Have you ever had the experience of driving to a destination confident of where you were, and then discovering you were going the wrong way? It happens to me a lot since I don't have a good sense of direction anyway. The result of my misdirection is being late for an appointment or meeting.

Life is a journey that also has a right and wrong direction. But this journey has more at stake than just being late. If we don't find our way quickly, it could be our death. Read Proverbs 14:12 again. Notice that the man thinks he's taken the right road. He walks along in perfect confidence that his destination is just ahead. After all, the road is wide with multicolored flowers on each side. The birds sing sweetly above his head and the smell of honeysuckle fills the air. Surely this road leads to a good place, he thinks to himself. However, being lost spiritually is a serious matter. This concept is so important that it appears again in Proverbs 16:25.

There are many signs along the way that tell us "Enter here, this is the way," but sadly, we've been deceived. Some of those road signs advertise false religious systems, secular and godless living, and humanism.

Scripture tells us that the road to eternal joy is narrow, but the road to destruction is wide. It tells us that the only true roadmap is found in the Bible. The beginning of a successful trip starts with a healthy fear and respect of Jehovah God (Psalms 111:10).

All believers are on a journey to find the right path in regard to every aspect of living. By reading, knowing, and studying the Word of God, we can avoid those roads that lead us in the wrong direction.

Pomp and Circumstance

"So, on the next day when Agrippa came together with Bernice amid great pomp, and entered the auditorium accompanied by the commanders and the prominent men of the city, at the command of Festus, Paul was brought in" (Acts 25:23).

The auditorium was filled with important dignitaries and prominent men residing in Caesarea. They had been invited to view the hearing of a man named Paul. The man had been the cause of great disturbances and mass mob violence in Jerusalem. The religious leaders in Jerusalem had accused Paul of dissension against the Jewish faith and stirring up the people in rebellion. Paul had been brought as a prisoner to Caesarea for his safety, and so that Felix, the Roman governor, could examine him to see what manner of complaint these charges were.

Felix had heard Paul's version of the incident in Jerusalem and could find no basis for the mob to demand Paul's death. Felix found Paul to be a fanatic about his beliefs, but could find nothing to warrant such a response from the religious leaders in Jerusalem. Since Felix was expecting a visit from another Roman governor named Agrippa and his sister, Bernice, Felix decided to allow them to hear this rebellious Jew and see what Agrippa might say.

As a hush settled over the auditorium, a palace guard loudly announced the entrance of Felix, Agrippa, and Bernice. Three seats had been set on a platform for the royal threesome.

Mary Baird

Bernice was arrayed in layers of woven linen material in multiple hues of blue that flowed around her as she walked with pride to the plinth. Her magenta head piece of tightly knotted flax was fashioned with silver coins. The two men wore brilliant red robes decorated with gold thread. Their robes were layered over ashen tunics. Jeweled crowns set in solid gold adorned their heads.

Several of the attendees in the back of the massive room whispered together in low tones. "I heard that Bernice was once married to her own uncle." One guest mumbled as she raised an eyebrow and furrowed her brow.

"Oh, that's nothing," said another, "I hear she and her brother, King Agrippa, are living as man and wife."

"I hear she'll do whatever is necessary to live a privileged lifestyle," said a third attendee.

The sharp sound of a court guard pounding the floor with his baton brought a deafening silence. "Bring in the prisoner," the guard loudly demanded.

A door opened from a side entrance and for a minute, no one emerged. Finally a prison guard stepped forward holding the arm of a small and insignificant looking man. He was clothed in burlap and had a rope for a belt. His gray hair and beard needed attending, but he walked with poise. The gathered dignitaries strained to see the man over the heads of those in front. *Who is this beleaguered looking man*, they whispered together, *that he should be called here?*

***

Bernice had been married several times—once to her uncle. She would marry, divorce (or leave her husband) to return to her brother, King Agrippa, with whom she carried on an incestuous relationship. At one time she was mistress to the Roman emperor, Titus. All of Roman society knew of her escapades. It's the stuff famous people are so well known for. Agrippa was the great grandson of Herod the Great who attempted to kill Jesus when he was a baby. Agrippa's father killed the Apostle James and tried to have the Apostle Peter killed also. This was not a family of distinction.

Paul had been called by God to preach the risen Lord and Savior Jesus Christ. He wanted his own people, the Jews, to realize that their Messiah had finally come. They had crucified him, but Paul wanted them to know that if they repented and accepted Jesus, they would be forgiven. Paul was willing to withstand the humiliation and even to die for his Lord. And so he stood before these dishonorable Roman rulers to be judged.

If we had been in that room on that day, which one would we have been honored to stand beside—the royal threesome on the platform or the lowly prisoner, Paul? We're certain where Paul is today, and we can know with surety where Felix, Agrippa, and Bernice reside.

We live in a world with a celebrity mentality. People clamor after the rich and famous. We pay our stars—of the movies, music, or sports—enormous sums of money. We make allowances for the worst kind of behavior toward those who are our idols, while those who live godly and moral lives receive no such acclaim. And in some instances the godly are ridiculed. Do we judge people by how they look and their popularity, or as God judges—by their hearts?

More than Esther's Story

> "All the king's servants and the people of the king's provinces know that for any man or woman who comes to the king to the inner court who is not summoned, he has but one law, that he be put to death, unless the king holds out to him the golden scepter so that he may live. And I have not been summoned to come to the king for these thirty days" (Esther 4:11).

The young Persian boys sat spellbound as Harbona paused in his story, "Tell us more, honorable one, please tell us more," their eyes sparkled with anticipation. "Don't leave us wondering. How did the beautiful queen escape death?" the boys continued their plea, "and what became of Haman?"

The old eunuch smiled, showing several missing teeth. "Well, let's see. Where did I leave off?"

Hamid spoke up quickly, "You said Queen Esther requested an audience with King Ahasuerus to tell him of Haman's plot to kill all the Jews in every province of Persia by an edict of the king. No one was allowed to go before the king—even his wives—unless they had been summoned by him."

"Yes, that's right," chimed in Mohsen, "but Esther was so beautiful that surely the king would not have ordered her killed, would he?"

Come, Let Us Reason Together

"You're correct, young ones, Esther was the most beautiful of the entire harem. I remember the first time I saw her when she arrived at the royal palace. She was so frightened and shy. Her attendant, Hegai, took special notice of her and when it was time for her to be presented before our king, she was magnificent. Of course, Queen Vashti was also beautiful; but because of her defiance toward the king, she was sent away in disgrace. Our king was so angry with her that he quickly ordered all the young, beautiful girls brought before him so he could select a new queen. No one knew at the time that Esther was Jewish. Her uncle, Mordecai, told her to keep silent about her lineage. However, no matter how beautiful Esther was, the king could have ordered her to be put to death."

"Why did Haman hate the Jews—especially Mordecai?" Sepehr wrinkled up his nose, then swatted a fly from his foot.

Harbona leaned closer to the group of young boys sitting in front of him. "It's probably because Mordecai wouldn't bow down and pay homage to him. When the servants assembled before Haman, Mordecai the Jew was the only one in the room not bowing. This made Haman so angry that he not only wanted Mordecai dead, but all the Jews as well. He was able to gain authority from the king to kill every Jew. Then, as a special 'treat,' Haman ordered a gallows built on which to hang Mordecai."

"Go on, go on—quickly tell us what happened next."

"Yes, yes" all the boys raised their voices together.

Harbona lifted his hand for silence. "One night when the king could not sleep, he had his servants read from the book of records and discovered that Mordecai the Jew had discovered a plot by some evil men to kill King Ahasuerus and warned the king's servants. The plot was overturned, and the king was safe. At the time, no one told the king the name of the man who saved him, but it had been recorded in the records, and that very night the king found out about Mordecai. The next day, Haman came to tell the king of his plan to hang Mordecai. But before he had the chance, the King told Haman he would be in charge of honoring Mordecai by giving him a royal robe and a crown and riding him through the city square. This honor would honor Mordecai for saving his life.

The boys fell on the ground in laughter. "I bet Haman was glad he hadn't told the king about the gallows he was building for Mordecai. What did Haman do then?" Mohsen asked, still chuckling.

Harbona stood up, grabbed his walking stick to steady himself, and winked at the boys. "You'll have to wait until tomorrow for your answer, Mohsen. It's time for me to rest, but I will tell you this—those Jews were sure lucky."

***

I imagine some might look at this story and think the same as Harbona. Those Jews were sure lucky. Mordecai had been taken captive when Babylon captured and ransacked Judah. He and his niece, Esther, lived in Susa under the rule of the Medo-Persian Empire. Several years earlier, the Jews were allowed to return to their homeland so they could rebuild the temple and worship Jehovah God. In defiance of God's desire for all Jews to return, many made the decision to stay in Babylon, and Mordecai was one of those Jews.

I'm aware that believers are told Esther and Mordecai are people we should emulate, but perhaps we need to take a closer look. The book of Esther is the only book in the Bible in which God's name is not mentioned. In fact, it's not recorded that Esther or Mordecai ever prayed! Maybe a better stand by Mordecai would have been to refuse to allow Esther to debase herself by becoming one of a heathen king's concubines. No one quotes from the book of Esther in the New Testament, and neither her name nor Mordecai is mentioned in the hall of faith as listed in Hebrews 11. And yet God is behind the scene working His miracles to protect the Jews in this foreign land from becoming extinct.

We know that God made a promise to Abraham as recorded in the book of Genesis and that contract or covenant will be honored by God. The Jewish people have been disciplined by God through the ages because of their unbelief, but eventually in time, they will inherit everything they were promised.

Is it possible that in this little book with these back sliding Jews—God is showing us something magnificent? Perhaps God is showing us His faithfulness to those who belong to Him even when their lives are not reflecting what we say we believe. I'd like to think that Esther and Mordecai did turn to God when their lives were on the line. Sometimes it takes that kind of situation to cause us to look up. As believers, we sometimes put God aside when things are going well for us. May we always keep before us the importance of a close walk with our Lord even in those times we think we need him less—so that in the bad times we won't have so far to walk.

Pleasing Prayer

"It happened that while Jesus was praying in a certain place, after He had finished, one of His disciples said to Him, 'Lord, teach us to pray just as John also taught his disciples'" (Luke 11:1).

The subject of prayer has been much talked about and little understood by many Christians. The teaching on prayer has gone the gamut of being used as a charm to receive desired pleasures from a benevolent God, to being considered a waste of time because we didn't receive what we wanted. Perhaps we will never truly understand the scope and power of prayer on this side of heaven, but as we study the Word, we may be able to sort through all the incorrect data and come to a true picture.

Four major aspects of prayer we can begin with are:

- Pray without ceasing (1 Thessalonians 5:17).
- Pray for one another (James 5:16).
- Pray believing (Matthew 21:22).
- Pray about everything (Philippians 4:6).

I thought it might benefit us to look at the prayer of a man who, in my opinion, had an understanding of the use and true purpose of prayer. In his letter to the church at Colossae, Paul begins by telling them something he prays ceaselessly for—them. It's found in Colossians 1:9-14. Get your Bible and we'll examine these verses to see Paul's heart regarding prayer for this body of believers.

The first thing Paul prays for his fellow believers is that they would be filled with the knowledge of God's will in true spiritual wisdom and understanding (Colossians 1:9).

We are told that "the fear of the Lord is the beginning of wisdom" (Proverbs 9:10). This concept must be implicit in our approach to this subject before anything else, and it is put into place the moment we comprehend through the Holy Spirit that we are a worthless, sinful person alienated from the sovereign God and destined for eternal separation and misery separated from His presence. Only then do we come to realize that there is but one remedy for our condition, and that remedy is the sacrificial work done on the cross by our Lord Jesus Christ. When we receive Him, we are on the road to discovering the true spiritual wisdom that the world neither knows nor cares about.

There is only one way for us to pursue this wisdom. There are no short cuts, no quick courses, and no absorbing it by osmosis. It is the study of the Word of God. We could spend weeks on this subject, but one verse stands out in my mind. "All Scripture is inspired by God and profitable for teaching, for reproof, for correction, for training in righteousness; so that the man of God may be adequate, equipped for every good work" (2 Timothy 3:16-17). As you read this reference, ask yourself: What is Scripture? How do the Scriptures work in my life? What do the Scriptures accomplish in me?

Paul, in our Colossians passage, tells his friends in Christ that there are three primary reasons why he prays for them to be filled with spiritual knowledge/wisdom. They are:

1. To live a pleasing life toward God on the earth.
2. To bear fruit for Him.
3. To increase our understanding of the One we worship.

A statement is made by our Lord in the Upper Room Discourse to His disciples on the eve of His death that has these same characteristics with very important implication for prayer. In John 15:7-8, He says, "If you abide in Me, and My words abide in you, ask whatever you wish, and it will be done for you. My Father is glorified by this, that you bear much fruit, and so prove to be My disciples."

Paul prays that these believers will recognize the strength and power they've been given by God so that they'll be steadfast in their walk, patient in their tribulations, and joyful in everything.

And why, Paul asks, shouldn't we be steadfast, patient, and joyful? God has made us fit to join the triune God in eternity, and to partake of our inheritance. Need we question the quality or magnificence of this inheritance? We cannot even fathom what is waiting for us in heaven!

Continuing in Colossians we see the ultimate mind-boggling—and majestic—work done for us through Christ. We, who were in total darkness and didn't even know it, have been removed from that pit of black death to the marvelous kingdom of Christ, and all the sins we committed in the past, present, and future have been forgiven. Note that Colossians 1:13 is written in the past tense. Although we are not there yet, God sees it as already accomplished. It only waits culmination.

Every time I read this prayer in Colossians, I feel as if I've been taken to the top of a mountain far above this earthly existence, and see once more the futility of making this life my utmost concern (1 John 2:15-17).

Therefore, how should we pray? God certainly wants us to come to Him with our every need, but if our prayers only consist of a list—even a good list—of worldly items we want Him to answer, I think we've missed an important aspect of prayer. When we pray as Paul did for the Colossians—and mean it—we may open up hardships for ourselves, and the ones for whom we intercede in order for God to bring about our request.

Very little spiritual truth is ever learned in an easy, sterile, and sedentary existence. The first chapter of Colossians closes with these words from Paul: "We proclaim Him, admonishing every man and teaching every man with all wisdom, so that we may present every man complete [mature] in Christ. And for this purpose also I labor, striving according to His power which mightily works within me" (Colossians 1:28-29).

Paul's passion for believers was that they grow and mature in Christ. I am forced to ask, as I pray for myself and others, if that is my passion. Is that what I labor for and strive to see accomplished through my prayers? May God rid us of a self-centered or self-gratifying prayer life.

Foolish Things

"But God has chosen the foolish things of the world to shame the wise" (1 Corinthians 1:27a).

When I was in high school, the senior class voted for a girl and boy they thought most likely to succeed in life. They were always the popular, good-looking ones, and a picture of them was prominently displayed in the pages of the yearbook. Years later when attending class reunions, it was interesting to learn that these chosen ones were often anything but successful. It turned out that some of the ones considered least likely to amount to anything often were the most successful in life.

There's a story in Judges 11:1-11 about a man named Jephthah of Gilead in Israel. He was a fierce warrior for his people, but he was the son of a harlot. Jephthah's father also had sons by his wife, and when they were grown, the true sons demanded that Jephthah leave their territory and never return. They swore that an illegitimate son would never share in the family inheritance. He fled to the land of Tob and became the leader of an army of other worthless men. We don't know for sure if these men were also outcasts and considered worthless, or if they were young and rebellious, but whatever the case, Jephthah was able to organize them into a band of fighting men.

It was during this time in Israel's history that the nation of Ammon harassed Israel to the point of destruction. The people of Gilead were unable to defeat them and they were in great distress. They swore that whoever could save them from this horde of murdering cutthroats would be their leader.

The people of Gilead had heard of Jephthah's vagabond army and so they sent the elders of the community to speak with Jephthah. No doubt, some of those elders were half brothers of Jephthah. He reminded them of how they had treated him and had thrown him out of their community. It doesn't say, but I have a feeling that Jephthah replayed every negative word and every cruel treatment he'd received at their hands. He agreed to fight for them on one condition—that they make him chief among the people. The elders willingly agreed to his request. You'll need to read more to find out the ending of this much debated and unusual story. But you cannot help but notice the number of times Jephthah mentions "The Lord, the God of Israel," and in Judges 11:29, it says that "the Spirit of the Lord came upon Jephthah." God was definitely using this illegitimate man for His purposes.

God has a standard of selection that is totally different from the way man selects. God chooses those that the world dismisses as insignificant. God has a good reason for his choosing: It's to remind us that we have nothing to brag about when it comes to our spiritual lives. We are told in 1 Corinthians 1:31b, "Let him who boasts, boast in the Lord." When I look at my own salvation, I can honestly say I am one of those foolish things. It's the one area of my life for which I am enthusiastically thankful.

Under His Wings

"He will cover you with His pinions, and under His wings you may seek refuge" (Psalms 91:4).

In Matthew 23:37-39, the Lord was grieving over Jerusalem because they had rejected all the prophets God sent them. And even though they had rejected God at every turn, Jesus is still longingly willing to forgive them.

In the previous verses, Jesus had issued eight woes toward the religious leaders in Jerusalem. They had become corrupt to the very top. Hypocrisy was their rule for living and they made life miserable for the common people. These leaders looked good on the outside, but inside they were rotten, smelly, dead men. The tragedy of it all was that they were not content to travel the road to destruction themselves; they were taking the nation with them. But in a tender moment, our Lord tells his people that he longed to gather them under His wings as a hen does her chicks, but they refused. Notice the result of their refusal. It's a powerful statement by our Lord.

We live in a stressful world filled with problems that can seem overwhelming. Family and friends may disappoint us; circumstances can change instantly. We look for comfort and answers many times in the wrong places. We can try to dull our pain with drugs, work, or material possessions, but these are all momentary solutions. The fears we sometimes face can be overwhelming to any human, and cynicism becomes our best friend.

Christians run to the Psalms for comfort and strength. Many of them were written by David and he knew about fear in a way we'll probably never experience. He was being chased by Saul, king of Israel, and many times David was only steps ahead of a man determined to kill him. David's writings give us the mind of a man who was often in despair, but maintained his faith in God.

Our Lord beckons us to trust Him and run for protection within His arms. He will never turn us away. David reminds us in Psalms 36:7, "How precious is Your lovingkindness, O God! And the children of men take refuge in the shadow of Your wings."

A young couple at our church body recently announced that they are going overseas as missionaries. The particular place they're going is extremely dangerous. They must follow stringent rules of behavior, and can never be sure that when they leave their residence they will return safely. I must admit that at first I found them irresponsible and my initial thoughts were negative. But as the husband explained that this was a mission God had placed on their hearts and that the couple were willing to take that chance, I realized that if this truly was God's plan, the couple would be as safe where they're going as a baby in the arms of its mother. Psalm 91:1 came to my mind: "He who dwells in the shelter of the Most High will abide in the shadow of the Almighty."

As believers, we can become sidetracked by the world. We begin to believe the lies our enemy, Satan, whispers in our ear. By the time we figure out that we've trusted in the wrong thing, our lives are filled with fear, and we forget that our Lord stands behind us with His arms open, waiting for us to rediscover His protective love. No matter what the circumstance, we are never safer than when we are under that shield.

Burning Hearts

"They said to one another, 'Were not our hearts burning within us while He was speaking to us on the road, while He was explaining the Scriptures to us?'" (Luke 24:32).

Within a body of believers, you will have a smorgasbord of disappointing developments. I've watched as men lost jobs, were out of work for a number of months, and then saw one hopeful possibility after another evaporate. I've seen young women longing to start a family miscarry over and over. I've seen parents of a teenager praying earnestly for their child to remember their Christian roots, only to be devastated time and time again. I've watched as death claimed loved ones at an early age. Anyone who thinks being a believer in Christ shelters you from trials hasn't read much Scripture or looked closely at Christians' lives. We battle spiritual doubts many times.

There's a story in Luke 24:13-35 about two men who were walking a dusty road in Israel toward the end of the day. They were sad and despondent. Neither man could think of anything positive to lift their spirits and give them hope. The events they discussed were enough to make anyone wonder if there was anything worth believing. Their whole world and all their dreams had fled into nothingness and futility.

Have you ever felt that way? Plans you worked so hard to bring about evaporated; people you had counted on for support walked away; sudden tragedies dismantled your security;

relationships were broken by misunderstandings or pride; and countless other dashed hopes and dreams have entered your life. I imagine we could all write a list.

Returning to our two men in Luke, we have a recording of their thoughts and why they were so despondent. As they journeyed, a third man joined them and walked along beside them. The third man sensed they were sad and were talking about some serious issues, so he asked them what they were discussing. Being shocked at his ignorance, they asked him where he came from that he didn't know all the events of the past three days. They related to the stranger that they had put all their confidence in a man who had claimed to be the Messiah. They had heard Him speak of God in a personal way as no man had ever done. They saw Him heal the sick, raise the dead, and restore sight to the blind; but His greatest message had been one of God's complete acceptance of them, and a glorious future in heaven. They envisioned Him overthrowing the Roman chains of slavery and restoring Israel to her greatness as it had been under King David.

But now, all was gone for these two men. Everything they had believed had not been fulfilled, and what was worse: this Prophet, this man who claimed to be from God, was dead. It was no ordinary death either—it was the humiliating death on a cross at the hands of the religious leaders in Israel. And that was not all! As if that were not enough, someone had stolen the body and hidden it. They were not even left with a place to visit to reflect on the man they loved and who had shown such love to them.

In the years I've walked this earth, it seems to me that when things were the most difficult, when I was tempted to give up, and when my faith was so weak that it made me ashamed—

that's the time when God moved in my life. Perhaps it's where He wanted me to be so that I'd realize that without Him, I could do nothing. When life is going great and we have successes, we tend to become overconfident. The Apostle Paul told us that he could do all things—*but don't miss the best part of that verse*—through Christ who strengthened him (Philippians 4:13). We must never forget the One who supplies us with our very breath.

Our story in Luke becomes interesting for us because we know that the third person is the resurrected Christ, but the two men didn't recognize Him. Their eyes were blinded, and they were too consumed with their own hurts to realize that the very one they had trusted, but thought was dead, was in their midst. Christ allowed the men to relate all their disappointments, fears, and worries. For a brief moment, He becomes their psychiatrist, so to speak. He allowed them to vent all their frustration.

I've found in my own life that I often vent to everyone but Christ when I'm faced with a problem too big to handle, rather than going to the one person equipped to offer me hope and encouragement. I forget that Christ has said He would never leave us nor forsake us, and that He would not only be with us, but in us. Just like those men on that dusty road, Jesus walks with me in the midst of my disappointments.

The next step in our story in Luke shows how the Lord corrects the defeatist attitude of these two men. Their belief had shifted to the material world rather than the spiritual world. They had forgotten everything Jesus had taught them during His ministry on earth and had replaced it with their own reasoning.

It's very difficult for me to keep my eyes and thoughts where they should be when times of testing come into my life.

Mary Baird

Scripture tells us that trials are designed to strengthen and grow us up spiritually (James 1:2-4). Faith grows under stress as we keep before us the precious promises found only in the Word of God.

Jesus explained to these two disciples that His death was not a cosmic mistake and had been predicted in the Old Testament. After Jesus finished His lesson, He acted as if He would leave them. The disciples urged Him to remain with them and share a meal.

When life is hard, do we long to be in fellowship with our Lord, or do we shut Him out? Do our fears drive Christ away, or pull Him closer? Worse still, do we blame Him for not caring about us and doubt His love? I confess I've been guilty of all three.

The next event in our story is riveting. Jesus replays the last supper before their very eyes, and when that happens, the blinders are lifted and they see Jesus for the first time. Just as quickly as Jesus appeared to them on the road, He vanished. Both men made a remarkable observation. They remember that as Jesus was explaining Scripture, their hearts burned within them. The previous feelings of dismay and discouragement vanished and their journey became one of joy. They immediately returned to Jerusalem to tell their brothers the good news of the Lord's resurrection.

Oh, that our hearts would burn within us as we read the good news of salvation in Christ, and share that with others. When fear enters our life, we have the greatest defense God could offer—His Word of hope.

Oh, Be Quiet!

"The heavens are telling of the glory of God; and their expanse is declaring the work of His hands. Day to day pours forth speech and night to night reveals knowledge. There is no speech, nor are there words; their voice is not heard" (Psalms 19:1-3).

I'll admit that I'm a talkative female. I have a feeling that there are times my husband wishes the remote control worked on me and he could press mute and shut me up. Many times I'm talking when I should be listening. I think the first few verses of Psalms 19 are saying the same thing.

It is estimated (and only an estimate) that there are between 10 sextillion to 1 septillion stars (give or take one or two), and between 100 billion to 1 trillion galaxies in our universe. The nearest galaxy of significance to ours is the Andromeda Galaxy. It is 2.5 million light years away but since we can't travel at the speed of light, you can see that we'd need to take several changes of clothes.[6]

We live in a time of artificial lighting. Everything has some kind of light. When I get out of bed before daybreak, I can see

---

6. Frasier Cain, information was originally published on Universe Today from three articles. http://www.universetoday.com/24328/how-many-stars/; http://www.universetoday.com/30305/how-many-galaxies-in-the-universe/; http://www.universetoday.com/30289/andromeda-galaxy/ (Accessed January 10th, 2013).

my way through the house just from the light coming from my many digital clocks, my computer, and even from my TV's cable box. Our society has become increasingly metropolitan; people not only have bright lights from the tall buildings, but even our streets are lined with poles of luminous bulbs. Because of all the artificial lighting, we cannot see the glory of the heavens. It's been many years since I was able to be in the open country on a clear night, look up, and see what has been up there all the time, but was hidden from my eyes.

Psalm 19 is telling us that it's a good idea from time to time to look up and see the handiwork of God. His massive power is always there for us to study and learn more about the majesty of our God. I've heard that in space it is deathly quiet. No talking is necessary. All the hustle and bustle of life melts into nothingness and only the witness of creation is heard.

We are told that the creation of the heavens was only finger work to God (Psalms 8:3-4). Our little planet Earth is not even on the radar when compared to the entire universe. If that doesn't make you shut your mouth, nothing will.

I fear we've settled for the artificial rather than the original, spiritually speaking. We've become so accustomed to living our lives in a fantasy world that we don't recognize reality. In many cases, Christians don't look much different from non-Christians. We've learned to imitate their life styles, their goals, their behavior, and even their entertainment.

Maybe it's time for a planetarium outing! Let's step up to the telescope, shut our mouths, and just look.

Our True Debt

"Owe nothing to anyone except to love one another; for he who loves his neighbor has fulfilled the law" (Romans 13:8).

The dreaded phone calls would begin around 8:00 at night. Since my husband traveled, I would often be the one to maneuver through the threats and harsh words from the stranger on the other end of the line. I longed for bedtime, but then once in bed, I'd toss and turn. We were Christians, but that didn't seem to have any practical meaning. Each day was the same. I kept a forced smile in front of my coworkers, and tried to escape my troubled mind by drowning in my work; fun and laughter were elusive. Such is the hollow existence of people experiencing a financial blow. The cause can be man-made or simply a matter of circumstances. Purchasing more stuff than you can afford, job loss, illness, and mismanagement of funds are just a few mistakes we can make, and sometimes it's a combination. No matter the cause, the results produce the same feelings of helplessness, worry, and sometimes panic.

What were we to do? Should we continue in the same mindset of constant frustration? Should we allow the situation to tear us apart? Financial problems often end with divorce. We knew that neither of those options had the approval of God. It certainly wouldn't be consistent with our testimony of trust in the Lord Jesus Christ. But the word "trust" had, by now, become a foreign concept. Any confidence I displayed toward others was manufactured.

I determined to increase the intensity of my prayers. After all, Scripture tells us to pray without ceasing and about everything. As Job in the Old Testament did when he lost everything—including his family and his health—I prostrated myself before the Lord and pleaded for help. Since we were falling behind on our mortgage payments, we needed to sell our house as quickly as possible. We listed our house with a realtor, but no one seemed interested.

It would make a lovely story if I could report that things began to look up for us, but within a few weeks after my increased earnest praying, my husband's business failed, and I was informed that my company was downsizing and my job would be ending in a short time. *Okay*, I thought, *what's going on here?* What was God trying to tell us? Was I going to have reservations about the love of God or His ability to do anything for us? Next I went through the phase of trying to figure out what we'd done to deserve such treatment by God.

I continued to search the Scriptures and discovered that many of God's people suffered terribly, and most of them were of more noble character than I was. What did leap out at me was the reassurance from God of His love and His constant vigil over His own. It appeared to me that the more heat placed on these people, the greater their faith became.

In Hebrews 11, the great chapter of faith, we see a list of faithful men and women who experienced various trials. Some were supernaturally delivered, but others were subjected to torture and execution. In the very next chapter, the writer states, "You have not yet resisted to the point of shedding blood in your striving against sin" (Hebrews 12:4). I hung my head and said, *No, I hadn't*. I added my own name to the beginning to drive the point home. You can add your own name there if you want.

It was at this point that I finally submitted myself, my problems, my family, whatever outcome, my life, my future and all that I had over to God. *Do with me as you will*, I told God. After all, I reasoned, to die only means being with the Lord sooner than later.

I've never experienced such peace as I did during those next few months. It seemed the more difficult things became, the more peace I experienced. I still had some bad days, but when I smiled, my smile was real, and when I laughed, my laugh was real. I felt a joy I couldn't explain.

Well, God didn't ask me to die for my faith. My job ended, but the owner decided to pay for all unused vacation and sick leave days over my 15 years. My severance pay was the exact amount needed to bring our house payments up-to-date. I found another job immediately. Through a friend's help, my husband also found a great job. We received a phone call from a realtor wanting to show our house to a client that was interested, and it sold. Within one year, we were debt free. God has shown me that He approves of debt, but the true debt He approves is our debt to love others, "Owe nothing to anyone except to love one another, for he who loves his neighbor has fulfilled the law" (Romans 13:8). We try to keep that in mind with our finances.

It's been many years since those events, and we've had other trials to face, but with each trial, our faith grows stronger. We know without a doubt that the Lord will never "leave us nor forsake us."

Questions for Reflection

1. What might be the worse outcome of your trial? Can you trust God for the very worst?

2. Psalms 55:22 tells us to cast all our burdens upon the Lord. Do you believe He's competent to handle your burdens?

3. Have you considered that God may use your demonstration of faith as a witness to others? (Romans 1:8)

About the Author

Mary Baird spent a thirty-five year working career in the area of finance and bookkeeping. After retiring a few years ago, Mary devoted her time between three passions—the study of God's Word, her family, and writing.

Mary began her publishing career with the *Upper Room* Magazine, of which she has been writing for the past few years. Additionally, Mary teaches a ladies' Bible study which has been an important part of her life for many years and a source of enjoyment in creating her own study outlines and handouts.

Through times of hardships and trials, Mary and her husband have seen God work in miraculous ways. Their marriage has been strengthened and they have persevered because they serve a faithful Savior.

More Titles by 5 Fold Media

The Transformed Life
by John R. Carter
$20.95
ISBN: 978-1-936578-40-5

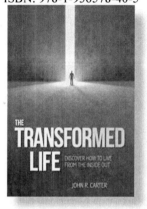

Personal transformation requires radical change, but your life will not transform until you change the way you think. Becoming a Christian ignites the process of transformation.

In this book, John Carter will teach you that God has designed a plan of genuine transformation for every person, one that goes far beyond the initial moment of salvation. More than a book this 10 week, 40 day workbook will show you how to change.

Luke, to the Lovers of God
The Passion Translation
by Brian Simmons
$14.95
ISBN: 978-1-936578-48-1

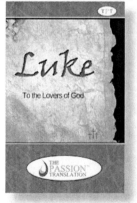

All four Gospels in our New Testament are inspired by God, but Luke's gospel is unique and distinct. Luke writes clearly of the humanity of Jesus—as the servant of all, and the sacrifice for all. In Luke's gospel, every barrier is broken down between Jew and Gentile, men and women, rich and poor. We see Jesus in Luke as the Savior of all who come to Him.

I highly recommend this new Bible translation to everyone.
~ Dr. Ché Ahn, Senior Pastor of HRock Church in Pasadena, CA

Like 5 Fold Media on Facebook, follow us on Twitter!

"To Establish and Reveal"
For more information visit:
www.5foldmedia.com

Use your mobile device to scan the tag above and visit our website.
Get the free app: http://gettag.mobi

CPSIA information can be obtained at www.ICGtesting.com
Printed in the USA
BVOW010208190313

315885BV00008B/19/P